To Harold and John,
who have always
appreciated our figures.

Table of Contents

Preface xi

Acknowledgments xv

Summary and Highlights xvii
   Wage Gap xvii
   Glass Ceiling xviii
   Pink Ghetto xix
   Female Entrepreneurs xx

PART I: Introduction 3

PART II: Women Are Closing the Gap 11
   Wages 11
   The Wage Gap 12
   The Existence of the "Glass Ceiling" 18
   Educational Attainment and Educational Choices 22
   Labor Force Participation 27
   Occupational Choice and the Pink Ghetto 33
   Women in Business 37
   Elected Officials 39
   Voting Patterns 43

PART III: Women, Poverty, and the Government 51
   Measures of Poverty 51
   Women and Welfare Reform 59

PART IV: African American Women 65
   A Continuing Success Story 65

PART V: Evaluating Claims of Discrimination 73

    Standards of Evidence 74

PART VI: Conclusion 79

Appendix: Statistical Tables 83

Bibliography 107

Index 119

About the Authors 123

List of Figures and Tables

PART II: Women Are Closing the Gap

Figure 2-1	Estimated Average Usual Weekly Earnings of Women as a Percentage of Men's Earnings, 1974–1993	14
Figure 2-2	Female-Male Wage Ratios at Age 30, 1980 and 1991	15
Figure 2-3	Women as a Percentage of Total Employment by Occupation, 1983 and 1997	20
Figure 2-4	Unemployment Rates by Sex, 1940–1997	21
Figure 2-5	Percentage of Associate's Degrees Awarded to Women, 1966–1996	23
Figure 2-6	Percentage of Bachelor's Degrees Awarded to Women, 1920–1996	23
Figure 2-7	Percentage of Master's Degrees Awarded to Women, 1920–1996	24
Figure 2-8	Percentage of Doctoral Degrees Awarded to Women, 1920–1996	24
Figure 2-9	Percentage of First Professional Degrees Awarded to Women, 1961–1996	25
Figure 2-10	Percentage of Master's Degrees in Business Awarded to Women, 1956–1996	25
Figure 2-11	Percentage of Law Degrees Awarded to Women, 1956–1996	26
Figure 2-12	Percentage of Dentistry Degrees Awarded to Women, 1950–1996	26

Figure 2-13	Percentage of Medical Degrees Awarded to Women, 1950–1996	27
Figure 2-14	Percentage of Adult Women Who Work, 1940–1997	28
Figure 2-15	Distribution of Female Labor Force by Educational Attainment, 1952–1998	29
Figure 2-16	Percentage of Labor Force That Is Women, 1948–1998	29
Figure 2-17	Total Employment by Sex, 1948–1998	30
Figure 2-18	Full-Time Employment by Sex, 1968–1997	31
Figure 2-19	Part-Time Employment by Sex, 1968–1997	31
Figure 2-20	Percentage of Women in the Labor Force by Marital Status, 1947–1997	32
Table 2-1	Selected Occupations Less than 10 Percent Female, 1998	34
Table 2-2	Percentage of Women in Selected Occupations, 1970 and 1998	35
Figure 2-21	Number of Women-Owned Businesses, 1972–1997	37
Figure 2-22	Industry Distribution of Women-Owned Firms, 1996	38
Table 2-3	Summary of Women Candidates for U.S. Congressional Offices, 1968–1998	39
Table 2-4	Summary of Women Candidates for State Executive and Legislative Offices, 1974–1998	40
Figure 2-23	Number of Women Candidates for U.S. Congressional Offices, 1968–1998	41
Figure 2-24	Number of Women in the U.S. Congress, 1917–1999	41
Table 2-5	Summary of Women in the U.S. Congress, 1917–2001	42
Table 2-6	Differences in Voter Turnout for Presidential Elections by Sex, 1964–1996	44
Table 2-7	Differences in Voter Turnout for Nonpresidential Elections by Sex, 1966–1994	45

PART III: Women, Poverty, and the Government

Figure 3-1	Life Expectancy at Birth by Sex, 1920–1996	52
Figure 3-2	Percentage of Population below Poverty Line by Sex, 1966–1997	52
Figure 3-3	Median Age at First Marriage by Sex, 1947–1998	55
Figure 3-4	Divorce Rates per 1,000 Married Women, 1920–1997	55
Figure 3-5	Marital Status of Women, Percentage Distribution, 1950–1998	56
Figure 3-6	Births per 1,000 Unmarried Women Ages 15–44, 1940–1996	57
Figure 3-7	Births per 1,000 Women Ages 15–44, 1940–1996	57
Figure 3-8	Percentage Distribution of Families with Children under 18 by Family Head, 1950–1998	58

PART IV: African American Women

| Figure 4-1 | African American and White Women's Earnings as a Percentage of Men's, 1967–1997 | 66 |

Figure 4-2	Female Percentage of Total Associate's Degrees Awarded to African Americans, 1977–1996	66
Figure 4-3	Female Percentage of Total Bachelor's Degrees Awarded to African Americans, 1977–1996	67
Figure 4-4	Female Percentage of Total Master's Degrees Awarded to African Americans, 1977–1996	67
Figure 4-5	Female Percentage of Total First Professional Degrees Awarded to African Americans, 1977–1996	68
Figure 4-6	Female Percentage of Total Doctoral Degrees Awarded to African Americans, 1977–1996	69
Figure 4-7	Median Income of African American and White Women, 1948–1997	69
Figure 4-8	Percentage of Female High School Graduates in the Labor Force by Race, 1959–1998	70

APPENDIX: Statistical Tables

Table A2-1	Estimated Average Usual Weekly Earnings of Women as a Percentage of Men's Earnings, 1974–1993	83
Table A2-2	Female-Male Wage Ratios at Age 30, 1980 and 1991	83
Table A2-3	Women as a Percentage of Total Employment by Occupation, 1983 and 1997	84
Table A2-4	Unemployment Rates by Sex, 1940–1997	84
Table A2-5	Percentage of Associate's Degrees Awarded to Women, 1966–1996	85
Table A2-6	Percentage of Bachelor's Degrees Awarded to Women, 1920–1996	85
Table A2-7	Percentage of Master's Degrees Awarded to Women, 1920–1996	86
Table A2-8	Percentage of Doctoral Degrees Awarded to Women, 1920–1996	86
Table A2-9	Percentage of First Professional Degrees Awarded to Women, 1961–1996	87
Table A2-10	Percentage of Master's Degrees in Business Awarded to Women, 1956–1996	87
Table A2-11	Percentage of Law Degrees Awarded to Women, 1956–1996	88
Table A2-12	Percentage of Dentistry Degrees Awarded to Women, 1950–1996	88
Table A2-13	Percentage of Medical Degrees Awarded to Women, 1950–1996	89
Table A2-14	Percentage of Adult Women Who Work, 1940–1997	89
Table A2-15	Distribution of Female Labor Force by Educational Attainment, 1952–1998	90
Table A2-16	Percentage of Labor Force That Is Women, 1948–1998	91
Table A2-17	Total Employment by Sex, 1948–1998	91
Table A2-18	Full-Time Employment by Sex, 1968–1997	92

Table A2-19	Part-Time Employment by Sex, 1968–1997	92
Table A2-20	Percentage of Women in the Labor Force by Marital Status, 1947–1997	93
Table A2-21	Number of Women-Owned Businesses, 1972–1997	94
Table A2-22	Industry Distribution of Women-Owned Firms, 1996	94
Table A2-23	Number of Women Candidates for U.S. Congressional Offices, 1968–1998	94
Table A2-24	Number of Women in the U.S. Congress, 1917–1999	95
Table A3-1	Life Expectancy at Birth by Sex, 1920–1996	96
Table A3-2	Percentage of Population below Poverty Line by Sex, 1966–1997	97
Table A3-3	Median Age at First Marriage by Sex, 1947–1998	97
Table A3-4	Divorce Rates per 1,000 Married Women, 1920–1997	98
Table A3-5	Marital Status of Women, Percentage Distribution, 1950–1998	99
Table A3-6	Births per 1,000 Unmarried Women Ages 15–44, 1940–1996	100
Table A3-7	Births per 1,000 Women Ages 15–44, 1940–1996	100
Table A3-8	Percentage Distribution of Families with Children under 18 by Family Head, 1950–1998	101
Table A4-1	African American and White Women's Earnings as a Percentage of Men's, 1967–1997	102
Table A4-2	Female Percentage of Total Associate's Degrees Awarded to African Americans, 1977–1996	102
Table A4-3	Female Percentage of Total Bachelor's Degrees Awarded to African Americans, 1977–1996	103
Table A4-4	Female Percentage of Total Master's Degrees Awarded to African Americans, 1977–1996	103
Table A4-5	Female Percentage of Total First Professional Degrees Awarded to African Americans, 1977–1996	104
Table A4-6	Female Percentage of Total Doctoral Degrees Awarded to African Americans, 1977–1996	104
Table A4-7	Median Income of African American and White Women, 1948–1997	105
Table A4-8	Percentage of Female High School Graduates in the Labor Force by Race, 1959–1998	106

Preface

A major thesis of popular media culture is that women are victims of their social condition. According to that theory, women suffer from substantial discrimination that leaves them less well-off than men. The apostles of this women-as-victims perspective use selected statistics and anecdotes to illustrate their theory. For example, women are depicted as earning consistently less than men. The corollary to that theory is that only government intervention can eradicate such discrimination to achieve parity between men and women.

Our intention in writing *Women's Figures* is to challenge several prevalent misconceptions about American women's economic opportunities. In debunking the familiar feminist tropes about women in the workplace—the glass ceiling, the wage gap, the pink ghetto—we hope to move the debate about women's economic progress forward by revealing the faulty methodological assumptions behind the "conventional wisdom" on this subject. We also want to highlight some of the many areas where women have made considerable gains: in education, in entrepreneurship, and in electoral politics, for example.

We conclude that complaints about systematic economic discrimination against women simply do not square with the evidence. Nevertheless, such claims continue to gain a hearing. In January 1999, President Clinton stated that "women earn about 75¢ for every dollar a man earns." In 1998 media nationwide uncritically reported on a new study by the research organization Catalyst that claims that women in the upper echelons of corporate America face a formidable wage gap. Every year, the Institute for Women's Policy Research publishes a state-by-state wage-gap study, which makes similar accusations about discrimination against women in the work force. Each of these claims fails to adjust for such crucial factors in determining wages and advancement as occupation, position, age, experience, education, and consecutive years in the work force.

Moreover, major organizations such as the National Organization for Women (NOW) and the Feminist Majority Foundation continue to claim that women do not enjoy equality of opportunity in the workplace. Their websites and literature warn women of the rampant "stealth discrimination" they face on the job. In Professor Deborah Rhode's book, *Speaking of Sex: The Denial of Gender Inequality* (Harvard University Press, 1997), she claims that "on almost all measures of social, economic, and political status, significant gender inequality persists."

To counter such common myths about women in the workplace, *Women's Figures* offers an accessible interpretation of data comparing women and men in America. Weaving those data together with explanations of the empirical evidence, we show how women's wages and education levels are closing the gap with those of men; how occupational choices, experience, and intensity of work effort have influenced wages; and how African American women have overcome enormous legal and social obstacles. An appendix provides a full set of data points, and an extensive bibliography offers a wide range of source material for those who wish to explore these issues further.

The evidence on the status of women in society is far more complex than the women-as-victims theory can explain. Women have made substantial progress in labor markets as a result of changes in technology, social attitudes, and laws. In many cases where women remain behind men, personal choices explain outcomes more readily than does overt discrimination. Even where discrimination may exist, we find little, if any, evidence that expanded government intervention would serve any useful purpose.

In the process of examining women's economic progress, we are struck by the pace of change in women's lives. We are also encouraged by the continued expansion of the debate over the effects of these changes on women and on men. Every month brings broader and more fruitful discussions about women and the workplace. Balancing work and family, implementing flextime and telecommuting options, and taking advantage of emerging opportunities for entrepreneurship are just some of the issues that now frequently arise in public debate. As our figures document, women's educational horizons continue to expand, and women are extending their reach in the professions and in political life. Although challenges remain, the achievements we document in this volume reveal the historically unparalleled freedom American women enjoy.

Acknowledgments

*W*omen's Figures reflects the efforts of many individuals at the American Enterprise Institute and the Independent Women's Forum. Audrey Williams of AEI patiently and conscientiously constructed the graphs, collected and updated each data series, reconciled inconsistencies in the text, kept track of different versions of the manuscript, and incorporated numerous changes. This book could not have been completed without her.

Leigh Tripoli of AEI meticulously and professionally edited the entire volume, provided invaluable suggestions on both content and presentation, and transformed our manuscript into a polished book. We were fortunate to have had access to an editor of her caliber and experience.

Allyson Brown of AEI designed the layout and cover and produced the figures and tables. We are indebted to her for complying with many last-minute requests.

Debra Coletti of Colby College, an AEI intern, reviewed every data point for errors and revisions and checked every footnote with the original source. She is to be congratulated for the number of errors she discovered; any remaining ones are our own.

Special thanks go to those who took the time to read and comment on the work, including Karlyn Bowman and Marvin Kosters of AEI, Arlene Holen of the U.S. Congressional Budget Office, Amy Holmes of the Independent Women's Forum, June O'Neill of the City University of New York, and Wendy Lee Gramm, former chairman of the Commodity Futures Trading Commission and board member of the Independent Women's Forum. Their insightful comments vastly improved both the structure and the message.

The authors would also like to thank Christopher DeMuth, AEI president, and David Gerson, AEI executive vice president, who made resources available for the project's completion.

This project would not have been started—nor completed—without Barbara Ledeen and Anita Blair of the Independent Women's Forum. Their support, drive, and encouragement are much appreciated.

Summary and Highlights

▮▯▯▮ Wage Gap

98¢: The Disappearing Wage Gap . . .

■ Data from the *National Longitudinal Survey of Youth* show that among people ages twenty-seven to thirty-three who have never had a child, women's earnings approach 98 percent of men's earnings.

■ Women's success has markedly increased over time. Between 1960 and 1994, women's wages grew ten times as fast as men's wages.

■ According to Professor June O'Neill, "When earnings comparisons are restricted to men and women more similar in their experience and life situations, the *measured earnings differentials are typically quite small.*"

Women Are Quickly Closing In

Women will continue to enter previously male-dominated, higher paying fields such as engineering, accounting, medicine, and law.

Q & A

What about the other two cents?

The two-cent difference might be accounted for by discrimination not yet eliminated, by differences between men and women that are unaccounted for, or by other factors not included in the studies.

Why do most figures on the wage gap claim a larger wage difference, usually about seventy-four cents for every male dollar?

Those comparisons fail to take into account underlying factors such as field of employment, work experience, continuous years in the labor force, daily hours of work, and personal choices.

▮▯▮▯ Glass Ceiling

Shattering the Glass Ceiling Myth

■ A Korn/Ferry study of the achievement of women over the past decade found that the number of corporate boards with women rose from 11 percent in 1973 to 53 percent in 1988 and 72 percent in 1998.

■ *The Glass Ceiling Commission Report* compared the number of women in the total labor force (without reference to experience or education levels) with the number wielding power in *Fortune* 1000 companies. A more accurate study would have compared women in the qualified labor pool (which for senior management positions is typically an MBA and twenty-five years of work experience) with the number of women who have actually achieved such senior positions.

■ *The Glass Ceiling Commission Report* examined only the *Fortune* 1000 industrial and *Fortune* 500 service companies, which represent only a small portion of the economy, and neglected huge inroads that women have made in the American economy as a whole.

■ Statistics tend to support the "pipeline theory" of women's corporate advancement. Labor force participation rates reveal that women have been working in significant numbers for only about thirty years.

■ Women's job turnover declined in the 1980s, reducing time between jobs and unemployment and helping to propel women up the career ladder. Since 1980, unemployment rates for men and women have never diverged by as much as a percentage point.

■ The pink ghetto is hardly the dead end that affirmative action supporters claim. The Glass Ceiling Commission conceded, for example, that the top two economic sectors expected to grow considerably between now and the year 2005 are female-dominated, namely, service/trade/retail and finance/insurance/real estate. In the years to come, the "ghetto" is likely to be an oasis for many women.

Pipeline to the Future

As women continue to go "through the pipeline," steadily increasing their numbers in previously male-dominated educational fields and professions, more women will achieve senior management positions in business and other fields.

Q & A

Why should we have to wait for women to become CEOs on a par with men? Why can't women reach the top now?

Turn the question around. Is it reasonable to expect that a woman with only seven consecutive years of work experience (a woman who might have, for example, taken time away from work to raise a family) would surpass another woman or a man who has been working for fourteen consecutive years? In the executive suite, as in the general job market, experience pays.

▮▮▮▮ Pink Ghetto

What Parents Need Most: Options

■ "Even highly successful women frequently want to spend much more time with their young children than the sixty-hour weeks required by the corporate fast track will permit."— Professor Elizabeth Fox-Genovese

■ Many women choose to enter the "pink ghetto" because the jobs offer much-needed flexibility; job skills are also more likely to deteriorate slowly in those fields, allowing women to leave the work force for a time—to have children, for example—and still retain the skills needed to be viable job candidates when they return.

■ "Although pay in women's occupations has been found to be lower than pay in typically male occupations, this fact alone is not evidence of employer discrimination."—Professor June O'Neill

■ A 1997 study by Professor Claudia Goldin found that only about 15 percent of women questioned who received college degrees around 1972 were maintaining both career and family. Among those who have had a successful career, as indicated by income level, nearly 50 percent were childless. More recent graduates are increasingly combining career and family.

Flexing Our Options

More companies will find that flexibility enhances their work force capability. Both men and women benefit from flextime.

Q & A

Even if women are getting equal pay for equal work, the fact is that we're not getting equal work. Aren't we stuck in dead-end fields?

Simply because one can find a higher concentration of women in certain occupations, it does not necessarily follow that they are being discriminated against. Instead, it may reflect the needs of certain women to choose career paths that allow them flexibility in raising children without significant costs to their careers.

■ ı ı ▌ Female Entrepreneurs

In Numbers Too Big to Ignore

■ The Small Business Administration found that in 1997 women owned 8.5 million small businesses in the United States, employing more than 23.8 million people and generating receipts of $3.1 trillion in sales.

■ "Women-owned businesses are growing more rapidly than is the overall economy and are major contributors to the nation's economic health and competitiveness."—Laura Henderson, National Foundation of Women Business Owners

■ Given present gains, levels of accomplishments, and rates of growth, female entrepreneurship will continue to flourish, and women business owners will become an even more important force in the economy.

Q & A

Do women-owned businesses receive government contracts?

Government contracts are primarily made with publicly traded corporations, which have significant female ownership. Women also benefit from special government set-aside programs for minorities and women. Most women-owned businesses are concentrated in the service sector.

PART
I

Introduction

*T*his volume analyzes women's condition in American society and challenges some enduring assumptions about women's social and economic progress. The book makes no effort or claim to be exhaustive in the topics it covers or the information displayed for each topic; instead, we present data that illustrate the difficulty in constructing plausible—much less conclusive—evidence from economic outcomes to support claims that American women are second-class citizens.

The book also gives a statistical rendering of the often-neglected historical record of women's progress. An examination of historical patterns in voting, marriage, education, employment, and other areas reveals the momentous though gradual changes that have taken place in American society. We have tried to provide figures from 1920 to the present. We believe that the year 1920 is an excellent starting point for mapping women's progress, for it was in that year, with the passage of the Nineteenth Amendment to the Constitution, that women achieved the right to vote. Since then, American women have achieved a great deal more.

One hundred years ago, American women were an unequal class in American society, complete with unequal laws, unequal schools, unequal access to political institutions, and unequal access to many jobs. Women not only could not enter some professions, but also could not own some forms of property. To find the causes of the inequality of women was simple: one needed to look no further than to federal, state, and local statutes, which in turn engendered unequal attitudes and expectations.

The twentieth century has witnessed many changes to the legal, social, and economic status of women. The inequality of institutions that characterized the early years of the century have largely vanished. Policymakers have removed the legal barriers to women's entering and participating fully in jobs and professions. Equality of opportunity now reigns. Employers in the United States may not engage in sex discrimination involving unequal pay for equal work or in discriminatory hiring or promotion practices.[1] Numerous court cases have upheld the statutes. In *Price Waterhouse* v. *Hopkins,* the Supreme Court ruled that Ann Hopkins, who had been denied a partnership at a major accounting firm, had been the subject of unfair discrimination. While some wage discrimination may persist, it does not appear to be pervasive in the American economy. The equality of opportunity that now exists is only partly the result of government intervention to remove legal barriers; it is also the result of nongovernmental forces such as changes in social attitudes that have come with time, changes in technology, and cultural reactions to those changes.

Our economy is at its most efficient with equality of opportunity. Without equality of opportunity for workers, outcomes are not truly competitive. Competition has led generations of Americans to strive for greater achievements not because outcomes were guaranteed to be the same, but because competition rewards effort, ingenuity, and capability regardless of the demographic characteristics of the participants. A competitive economy yields the greatest innovations and the most benefits for both consumers and producers. Competition, however, will lead to equality of outcome for workers only if they are truly identical in all respects. Identical outcomes are impossible in competitive markets to the extent that people differ.

Thus, equality of opportunity in America has not necessarily translated into identical job-related outcomes for women and men. Some observers of the status of women in America find nothing unnatural, unsettling, or unexpected in a wide range of disparate outcomes resulting from equal opportunity in a free and competitive society. Those observers do not see unequal outcomes as the necessary consequence of discrimination. Instead, they point to an array of explanations ranging from a transition from former discriminatory practices to differences in experience, education, and skills, as well as to differences in preferences, motivations, and expectations as reasons to expect nonidentical outcomes.

According to advocates of competition, *equal opportunity* should be the primary policy objective of government, since federal, state, and local governments currently provide American women with sufficient equal opportunity protections through a complex web of statutes and regulations. While isolated instances of sex discrimination occur, available statutes can remedy any harm. To those observers, American women—and, indeed, all Americans—benefit most from equal economic opportunity to participate in a free and open competitive economy without further intrusion from the government.

But other observers of the status of women in America see differences in outcomes as the failure rather than the efficiency of our economy. They do not believe that wages and jobs should necessarily be the product of free exchange between buyers and sellers, and they see the nonidentical positions of men and women in the United States as the result of a sinister system that is inherently unfair to women and in need of further government market intervention. Some claim that the failure to reach *equality of outcome* is evidence that opportunities are, in fact, not yet equal, that current legal remedies are inadequate, and that further government intervention is necessary.[2] Such observations have led to the claim that equality of outcome, rather than equality of opportunity, should be the goal for public policy, and consequently further government intervention is needed.

Still others believe that women are victims of their social condition.[3] According to those claims, women do not fully benefit from equal opportunity because many women accept social stereotypes that determine their preferences, motivations, and expectations. Thus, American women are denied the same rights, privileges, and opportunities as men as a consequence of American socialization. The suggested remedy is considerable government intervention on behalf of women.

Finally, some claim that a failure to reach equality of outcomes for men and women in America is simply an artifact of the failure of our economic system. Specifically, they contend that our economy does not reward women with their rightful wage. They assert, for example, that teachers should be paid as much as engineers. Those skeptics fail to recognize the legitimacy of simple differences. Instead, their common theme is that currently available legal remedies are inadequate and that further government intervention is necessary.[4]

A sampling of recent statements from some organizations gives the impression that American women are locked in a losing struggle with men in almost all areas of society.[5] According to those groups, women battle lower wages, compulsory occupational segregation, and the burden of a "glass ceiling," to name just a few. But the evolution of the American labor market demonstrates that women are closing the gap. That we discuss in Part Two. After showing how poverty disproportionately affects women in Part Three, we describe the success story of African American women in Part Four. In Part Five we analyze standards of evidence for sex discrimination and show why those standards ought to be higher for the indirect evidence proffered by the current advocates of women as victims. Part Six presents our conclusions.

NOTES

1. The Equal Pay Act of 1963 and Title VII of the Civil Rights Act of 1964 bar such discrimination.

2. See, for example, Deborah Rhode, *Speaking of Sex: The Denial of Gender Inequality* (Cambridge: Harvard University Press, 1997); Nadine Strossen, "Women's Rights under Siege," *North Dakota Law Review,* vol. 73 (1997), pp. 207–30. Gloria Steinem has claimed that expanded affirmative action policies are necessary to "rescue women who have fallen into a river of discrimination." See Karen DeWitt, "Feminists Gather to Affirm the Relevancy of Their Movement," *New York Times,* February 3, 1996, p. A9; see also Steinem's article, "Revving Up for the Next 25 Years," *Ms.,* September/October 1997, p. 82. See also "For Affirmative Action" by Faye J. Crosby and Sharon D. Herzberger in Richard F. Tomasson, Faye J. Crosby, and Sharon D. Herzberger, eds., *Affirmative Action: The Pros and Cons of Policy and Practice* (Washington, D.C.: American University Press, 1996).

3. For a recent example, see Sheila Tobias, *Faces of Feminism: An Activist's Reflections on the Women's Movement* (Boulder, Colo.: Westview Press, 1997); for a good analysis of this issue, as well as the debate between "gender feminism" and "equity feminism," see Christina Hoff Sommers, *Who Stole Feminism?* (New York: Simon and Schuster, 1994); see also, Elizabeth Powers, "A Farewell to Feminism," *Commentary,* January 1997, pp. 23–30.

4. In this context, a skeptic holds the view that women's outcomes are the result of discrimination rather than economic supply and demand characteristics.

5. See, for example, a statement by National Organization for Women (NOW) President Patricia Ireland, after NOW named Smith Barney a "merchant of shame": "Many businesses are 'doing business the old-fashioned way,' as Smith Barney puts it—they're still exploiting women." See NOW Press Release, "NOW Targets Smith Barney as First 'Merchant of Shame'; Calls All Employers to Take Women-Friendly Workplace Pledge," March 12, 1997. Affirmative action supporter Mary K. O'Melveny writes that "barriers to advancement remain substantial and pervasive." O'Melveny, "Playing the 'Gender' Card: Affirmative Action and Working Women," *Kentucky Law Journal*, vol. 84 (1996): 863–901; in a recent speech, ACLU President Nadine Strossen claimed that "without affirmative action, women will increasingly be relegated to lower paying occupations and positions, which will adversely affect their whole families." Strossen, "Women's Rights under Siege."

PART
II

Women Are Closing the Gap

*M*ost recent data indicate that women are closing the formerly wide gulfs that separated the sexes in terms of economic, social, and educational status. Here, we examine the narrowing gaps in wages, educational achievement, labor force participation, occupational choices, and election to public office.

Wages

In the 1960s protesters wore "59¢" buttons to publicize the charge that women earned only fifty-nine cents for every dollar earned by a male. Three decades later, some groups such as the National Organization for Women (NOW) claim that women are still punished with lower wages, earning somewhere between sixty to eighty-nine cents for every dollar earned by a male. Those claims, however, fail to recognize the multiple factors that affect income levels.

Employment compensation is perhaps the bloodiest battleground in the wars between the sexes. It is also the area in which the most blatant distortion of statistics has occurred. In particular, two rhetorical devices loom large over nearly every report on the subject of employment compensation: the "wage gap" and the "glass ceiling." Cited constantly by those skeptical of economic outcomes, such popular mantras have been used to argue that income inequality between the sexes is the direct result of discrimination on the part of employers and that government intervention is the only solution. The statistics and arguments deployed as evidence for the existence of both the "wage gap" and the "glass ceiling" do not, however, withstand close examination.

The Wage Gap

Frequently cited as evidence of sex discrimination in employment compensation is the "wage gap." The U.S. Department of Labor reports that the ratio of women's median weekly earnings to men's is 74 percent.[1]

Professor Sharon Oster has argued that such numbers, removed from their context, tell us little about the existence of discrimination. Specifically, they do not take into consideration important determinants of income. The "adjusted wage gap" between men and women—the difference in wages after accounting for differences in occupation, age, experience, education, and time in the work force—is far smaller than the "average wage gap," which is found by comparing averages of all men's and women's wages. The former is a more accurate description of differences.[2]

Although discrimination is frequently blamed for income differentials, a host of choices made by men and women—personal choices made *outside* the work environment—have important implications for men's and women's earnings. Those choices often have a negative effect on pensions, promotions, and total wages.

Recent economic literature on choices made by women in the working world emphasizes that multiple forces play an important part in determining compensation. Occupation, seniority, job turnover, and intermittent work force participation are all critical variables in accounting for pay disparities. In other words, those who assume that discrimination is solely to blame for wage differences are drawing unsubstantiated conclusions. The issue is far more complex.

Decisions that affect seniority and turnover are particularly important to understand. For example, 80 percent of women bear children at some point in their lives,[3] and approximately a quarter of employed women work part-time, so a higher percentage of women's work years are spent away from work. Hence, women's opportunities for promotion may not be so great as those of their male colleagues. That in itself is not evidence of discrimination, but of personal decisions women have made.

It is likely that women, who are most frequently children's primary care-givers, consider the responsibilities of motherhood when making employment decisions. Thus, as we noted earlier, many women, planning to interrupt their careers at some point in the future to have children, choose occupations where job flexibility is high, salaries are lower, and job skills deteriorate at a slower rate than others'. Furthermore, men and women choose different fields of study that result in different income levels after graduation. Since that is the case, comparing incomes by the highest degree earned does not measure discrimination and produces numbers that are politically useful but meaningless in practice. Given those educational and career choices, comparing the *average* wages of men and women is a misuse of statistics and a grossly misleading comparison.

Nevertheless, in 1998, Catalyst, a research organization, released a study allegedly showing that women are underpaid.[4] Catalyst examined salaries of officers in *Fortune* 500 companies and concluded that "women are facing another formidable obstacle: a wage gap at the top of corporate America," earning only $518,596 annually compared with $765,000 for their male counterparts, or sixty-eight cents on the dollar. When chief executives were excluded, that calculation left women earning seventy-seven cents for every dollar earned by a man.

The Institute for Women's Policy Research (IWPR) published a report in 1998 that showed state-by-state comparisons for women's pay.[5] According to the IWPR, women fare worst in Oklahoma and Alabama, where they earn approximately sixty-three cents on a man's dollar, and fare best in the District of Columbia and Maryland, where they earn eighty-seven and seventy-five cents, respectively. "In the worst states, it's really socked to women every payday," said Heidi Hartmann, executive director and president of the institute.

Those studies have received extensive press coverage, with reports on television, radio, and both major and regional newspapers, from the *Orlando Sentinal* to the *Des Moines Register* and the *Hartford Courant*. If the studies are to be believed, then American women remain second-class citizens. But, before declaring another crisis, it is worth examining some of the numbers behind the differences.

Figure 2-1 shows estimates of the ratio of average women's to men's earnings in three different age groups from a data series constructed by Professors David Macpherson and Barry Hirsch.[6] We can see that women's average wages have been rising relative to men's wages in all age groups over the period 1974 to 1993. The greatest gains for women have been in the youngest age group, age sixteen to twenty-nine, for whom wages rose from 77 percent to 92 percent over that period. It is significant that the younger the age group, the higher the average wage relative to men's. Data from the *National Longitudinal Survey of Youth* show an even smaller adjusted wage gap between men's and women's earnings: among people ages twenty-seven to thirty-three who have never had a child, women's earnings are close to 98 percent of men's.[7] As Professor June O'Neill noted, "When earnings comparisons are restricted to men and women more similar in their experience and life situations, the measured earnings differentials are typically quite small."[8]

Many studies document the link between increased numbers of children and decreased earnings. Professor Jane Waldfogel compared the adjusted wage gap between men and women with the

FIGURE 2-1

Estimated Average Usual Weekly Earnings of Women as a Percentage of Men's Earnings, 1974–1993

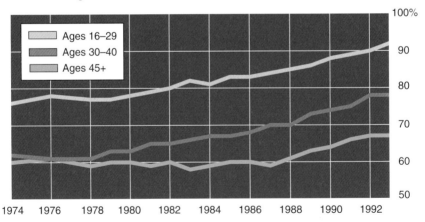

NOTE: Data for 1975 and 1977 are not available.

SOURCE: David A. Macpherson and Barry T. Hirsch, "Wages and Gender Composition: Why Do Women's Jobs Pay Less?" *Journal of Labor Economics*, vol. 13 (July 1995), p. 466, table A1.

same experience and education for mothers and women without children.[9] Figure 2-2 shows her results. Even in 1991, women without children made 95 percent of men's wages, all other factors accounted for, but mothers made 75 percent of men's wages. And the wage gap has shrunk between 1991 and 1999, as more women attend college and move into the labor force.

That finding appears again and again in the economic literature. Consider two more examples. Professors David Neumark and Sanders Korenman have published several papers analyzing ways of measuring the effects of marriage and motherhood on wages.[10] They found that, whereas marriage did not lower wages, having children did. The more children, the lower the earnings, all other factors equal. Professor Claudia Goldin found that few women achieved both career and family.[11]

Naturally, there are different explanations for those data. One is that children take time away from women's careers, both in terms of time out of the work force to bear the children and in terms of time put into work effort afterwards.

FIGURE 2-2

Female-Male Wage Ratios at Age 30, 1980 and 1991

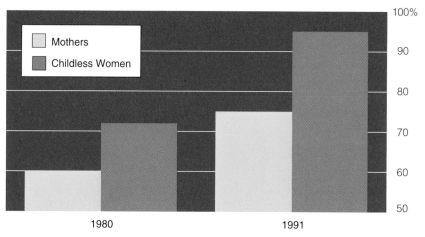

SOURCE: Jane Waldfogel, "Working Mothers Then and Now: Effects of Maternity Leave on Women's Pay," in Francine Blau and Ronald Ehrenberg, eds., *Gender and Family Issues in the Workplace* (New York: Russell Sage Foundation, 1997).

A second explanation is that women who invest in education to qualify for high-paying jobs—who major in business or math, or who acquire professional training, for example—choose to work and reap the returns from that education. They delay having children, have fewer of them, or have none at all.

A study by Professors Chinhui Juhn and Kevin Murphy buttressed that explanation. They found that the movement of women into the work force between 1969 and 1989 was dominated by those whose husbands earned the most—and who earned the most themselves.[12] Potential earnings rather than economic necessity drove women into the work force. In 1969 the earnings of wives tended to be the same across husbands' wage categories. Twenty years later, the wives of high-income husbands both worked longer hours and earned significantly more. By suggesting that the pull of higher wages lures women into employment, Juhn and Murphy's research contradicts the widely held view that women enter the labor force because they cannot afford to stay home. Professor Jacob Mincer first showed that in the early 1960s.[13]

Of course, many people would offer a third explanation: employers discriminate against women who have children. According to that argument, mothers are paid less for the same work or are forced into positions of lower responsibility. But if systematic discrimination of that type existed, firms hiring only mothers would make larger profits than others. In the same way, if women were paid only seventy-four cents on a man's dollar, then a firm could fire all its men, replace them with women, and have a cost advantage over rivals. Such a scenario occurs among neither male nor female employers, however.

Yet some people continue to promote discrimination as the primary cause of earnings differences between men and women. A survey of women lawyers demonstrates that reasoning. In a 1998 book, *Presumed Equal: What America's Top Women Lawyers Really Think about Their Firms*, authors Suzanne Nossel and Elizabeth Westfall claim that despite women's educational gains in law schools, their demonstrated success in garnering jobs in good law firms, and the significant increase in workplace acceptance, "systemic forces hold back women's progress and will continue to do so until institutional and societal changes are made."[14]

Just what those mysterious "systemic forces" are is unclear from the respondents in the survey. Nossel and Westfall admit that women associates reported that their chances of promotion were equal to those of men "provided they [were] willing and able to put in the long hours and enormous energy."[15] The authors also reported that attrition rates for women associates are higher than for male associates and that the most frequently cited reason for women's leaving law firms "relates to the difficulty of sustaining a law firm career once one has children."[16] Even some men, they noted, were "beginning to follow women out of firms" to have more time with their families.[17] In general, the women lawyers who responded to Nossel and Westfall's questions demonstrated "a keen awareness that the women who had achieved the greatest success in their firms did so at considerable personal cost."[18]

Nossell and Westfall's evidence, culled directly from female lawyers in law firms, provides evidence that the choices women make *outside* the workplace have significant consequences for their achievement *within* the workplace and that women, like men, can make it to the top—but not without sacrifice. What appears to be happening (and what those who cite discrimination ignore) is that women in many professions are making decisions to balance work and family priorities and that those decisions can result in fewer women's reaching the top of their fields.

Those who measure success solely by women's performance in the professional world rarely recognize that trend. Many mothers with small children give high priority to spending time with them and are willing to risk higher rates of absenteeism and thus fewer opportunities for promotions.

It may be unfair that the bulk of child-care responsibilities continues to fall to mothers rather than to fathers, but it is not clear that most women see motherhood as a burden. According to Professor Elizabeth Fox-Genovese, "Even highly successful women frequently want to spend much more time with their young children than the sixty-hour weeks required by the corporate fast tracks will permit."[19] The quandary many women face when they combine work and motherhood is a painful one, but it is a choice best made by the individuals involved. An increasing number of men are changing the schedules of their professional lives to have more time both for themselves and with their families.

A preference for more time at home with less pay and less job advancement over more time at work with more pay and advancement is a legitimate individual choice for women. Similarly, the choice of some men to retire early and forgo additional earnings, a continuing trend, does not prove inequality between young and old. One of the greatest harms that the feminist movement inflicted on American women was to send the message that women are *only* fulfilled if their salaries are equal to men's and that a preference for more time at home is somehow flawed. Neither men's nor women's education and job choices prove social inequality. In an ideal world a central authority does not mandate outcomes. Rather, men and women are free to pursue their dreams, both professionally and personally.

The Existence of the "Glass Ceiling"

Does the "glass ceiling" exist? Are American women systematically denied access to the upper echelons of professions simply because they are women? The *glass ceiling* was a term coined by the *Wall Street Journal* in 1986 to describe the "invisible but impenetrable barrier between women and the executive suite." It is alleged that the glass ceiling, like occupational segregation, prevents women from attaining the more lucrative positions.

The Civil Rights Act of 1991 created a Glass Ceiling Commission charged with monitoring and reporting on the diversity of the American workplace. The commission in 1995 released a report that has since become gospel to those claiming victim status for women. It ominously concluded that only 5 percent of senior managers at *Fortune* 1000 industrial and *Fortune* 500 service companies are women and implied that systematic discrimination was the cause.[20]

Yet an assessment of the Glass Ceiling Commission's methods raises questions about that 5 percent figure. Typical qualifications for corporate senior management positions include both an MBA and twenty-five years of work experience. The logical sequence of questions the commission should ask would be, first, What percentage of women meets these requirements? and, second, Of that group of qualified women, what proportion has made it to the upper ranks of corporate America? By comparing the number of women qualified to hold top executive positions with the number actually in those positions, one could make some conclusions about the existence of a "glass ceiling."

Those are not the questions the Glass Ceiling Commission asked, however. Instead, it compared the number of women in the total labor force, without reference to experience or education levels, with the number wielding power at large corporations. That comparison results in a statistically corrupt but politically useful figure of 5 percent. In its refusal to use the qualified labor pool in its assessment, the commission reached alarming but highly misleading conclusions about women's employment opportunities.

A cursory glance at the history of professional school degrees reveals that very few of the graduates of the 1950s and 1960s, who today would be at the pinnacles of their professions, were women. That lends support to the "pipeline" theory, which holds that women have not made it to the top in some professions simply because they have not been "in the pipeline" long enough to gain the requisite experience. In addition, since entering the work force in significant numbers, women have also steadily increased their numbers in "male-dominated" professions, as illustrated in figure 2-3. Critics attack the pipeline theory as an excuse for ignoring discrimination in the workplace, but women's gains in the American economy (as our analysis of women in business reveals) and in the corporate world show that the pipeline theory remains the most viable explanation for women's progress. The Korn/Ferry executive search firm found that in 1998 women were represented on 72 percent of major corporate boards. That is a major increase from 1988, when women were on 53 percent of boards, and an even more dramatic increase from 1973, when only 11 percent of corporate boards included women.[21] Yet critics of the pipeline theory ignore that remarkable growth and choose instead to focus on only the number of women in CEO positions.

FIGURE 2-3

Women as a Percentage of Total Employment by Occupation, 1983 and 1997

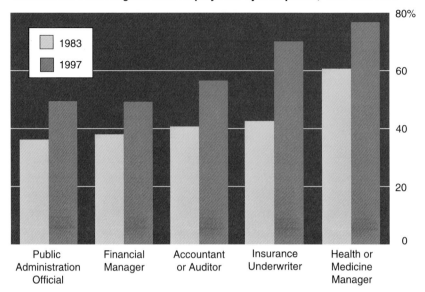

SOURCE: U.S. Department of Labor, Bureau of Labor Statistics, unpublished tabulation from the *Current Population Survey.*

The Glass Ceiling Commission concluded that the key factor preventing women's advancement is discrimination. "In the minds of white male managers," the report stated, "business is not where women of any race or ethnicity were meant to be—certainly not functioning as the peers of white men."[22] That is an alarming statement, but no evidence exists that such attitudes are pervasive in the business world. Indeed, the only evidence the report cites are two brief statements by male managers, neither of which suggests that women do not belong in the workplace.

Finally, it is worth noting that large corporations are only one portion of the market, and, given recent evidence of the success of women moving into previously male-dominated occupations, the conclusions of the commission say little about women's participation in the economy as a *whole.*

As the above discussion has demonstrated, both the *glass ceiling* and the *wage gap* are rhetorically powerful but factually bank-

FIGURE 2-4

Unemployment Rates by Sex, 1940–1997

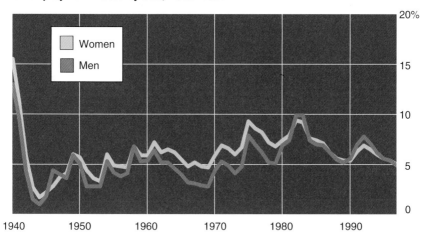

NOTES: Data beginning for 1994 are not directly comparable with earlier years. Data for 1940–1946 include ages fourteen and older; starting in 1947, data include ages sixteen and older. Beginning in January 1997, data reflect revised population controls used in the household.

SOURCES: *Historical Statistics,* vol. 1, D11-25, pp. 127–28. *Statistical Abstract:* 1950, no. 209; 1977, no. 627; 1979, no. 647; 1988, no. 647; 1991, no. 635; 1994, no. 616; 1995, no. 628. *Employment and Earnings:* January 1997, p. 193, table 24; January 1998, p. 196, table 24.

rupt terms. Those who insist on invoking such concepts as *evidence* of discrimination encourage unnecessary and harmful government intervention. Individual cases of discrimination still occur in the workplace, but laws prohibiting discrimination have been in existence for thirty years and should continue to be rigorously enforced. One should not, however, cite such occurrences as evidence of rampant discrimination. What we need to recognize, as Michael Lynch and Katherine Post have suggested, is that "[t]he differences that now exist are the result of individual choices, not of third-party discrimination."[23] Furthermore, salary levels are not the only consideration for workers. Flexibility, work setting, and job interest are important to both men and women.

Figure 2-4 presents the unemployment rates for men and women between 1940 and 1997. Since 1980, rates have never diverged by as much as a percentage point. This is so since women's job turnover declined significantly in the 1980s, reducing time between jobs and hence employment. Employment continuity and job commitment give women the best opportunity to move up to the executive suite.

Educational Attainment and Educational Choices

At the beginning of the twentieth century, education, particularly higher education, was aimed primarily at men. Many schools and colleges were exclusively for men. Many of the professions for which college provided preparation—such as divinity, law, medicine, and engineering—were by common practice (if not by law) restricted to men. Figures 2-5 through 2-8 illustrate the steadily growing percentage of associate, college, and graduate degrees awarded to women in the United States since 1920 (data for associate degrees begin in 1966).[24] Today, the majority of associate, bachelor's, and master's degrees are awarded to women, as well as 40 percent of doctorates.

Women have made considerable gains in education. Not only are women represented in greater numbers at the college and postgraduate levels, but they have also been steadily entering traditionally male-dominated programs. In 1999 women represented 44 percent of the freshman class at Yale Medical School and earned more bachelor's and master's degrees than men. According to data from the Department of Education, women have outnumbered men in both undergraduate and graduate school since 1984.[25] Figure 2-9 charts the dramatic increase in the percentage of first professional degrees awarded to women from 5 percent as recently as 1970 to 42 percent in 1996. Figures 2-10 through 2-13 show a similar pattern of the women's share of degrees awarded in each of the specific professional fields of business, law, dentistry, and medicine.

FIGURE 2-5

Percentage of Associate's Degrees Awarded to Women, 1966–1996

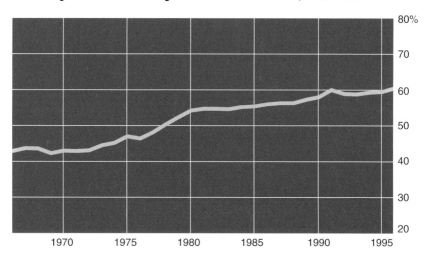

SOURCE: U.S. Department of Education, National Center for Education Statistics, Integrated Postsecondary Education Data System, "Completions" surveys.

FIGURE 2-6

Percentage of Bachelor's Degrees Awarded to Women, 1920–1996

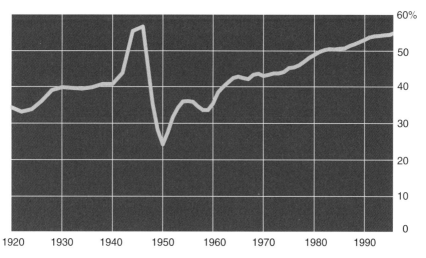

NOTE: Data for odd years from 1921 to 1947 are not available.

SOURCE: U.S. Department of Education, National Center for Education Statistics, Integrated Postsecondary Education Data System, "Completions" surveys.

FIGURE 2-7

Percentage of Master's Degrees Awarded to Women, 1920–1996

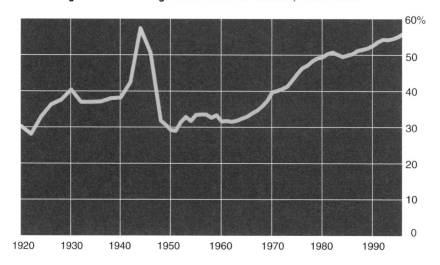

NOTE: Data for odd years from 1921 to 1947 are not available.

SOURCE: U.S. Department of Education, National Center for Education Statistics, Integrated Postsecondary Education Data System, "Completions" surveys.

FIGURE 2-8

Percentage of Doctoral Degrees Awarded to Women, 1920–1996

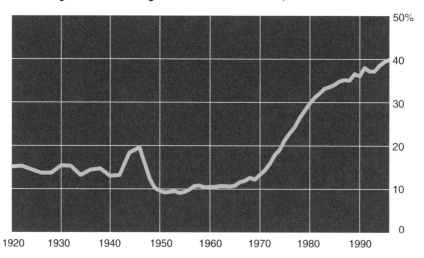

NOTE: Data for odd years from 1921 to 1947 are not available.

SOURCE: U.S. Department of Education, National Center for Education Statistics, Integrated Postsecondary Education Data System, "Completions" surveys.

FIGURE 2-9

Percentage of First Professional Degrees Awarded to Women, 1961–1996

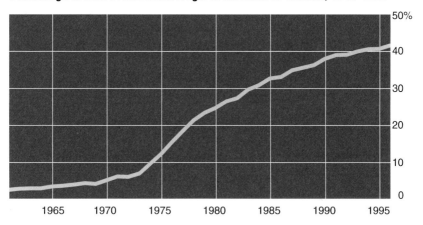

NOTE: First professional degrees are defined as requiring at least two years of college and a total of six years of schooling and certify an individual to practice a particular profession. First professional degrees are conferred in the fields of chiropractic medicine, dentistry, law, medicine, osteopathic medicine, pharmacy, podiatry, theology, and veterinary medicine.

SOURCE: U.S. Department of Education, National Center for Education Statistics, Integrated Postsecondary Education Data System, "Completions" surveys.

FIGURE 2-10

Percentage of Master's Degrees in Business Awarded to Women, 1956–1996

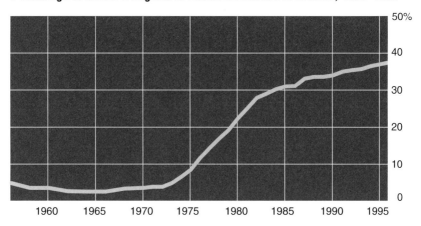

NOTE: Includes degrees in business management/administrative services, marketing operations/ marketing and distribution, and consumer and personal services. Data for odd years from 1957 to 1969 are not available.

SOURCE: U.S. Department of Education, National Center for Education Statistics, Higher Education General Information Survey, "Degrees and Other Formal Awards Conferred" surveys, and Integrated Postsecondary Education Data System, "Completions" surveys.

FIGURE 2-11

Percentage of Law Degrees Awarded to Women, 1956–1996

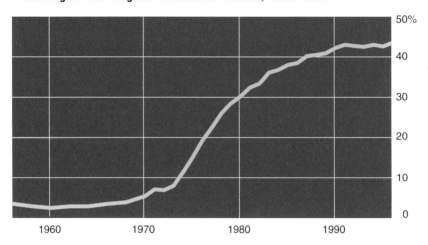

NOTE: Data for odd years from 1957 to 1969 are not available.

SOURCE: U.S. Department of Education, National Center for Education Statistics, "Degrees and Other Formal Awards Conferred" surveys, and Integrated Postsecondary Education Data System, "Completions" surveys.

FIGURE 2-12

Percentage of Dentistry Degrees Awarded to Women, 1950–1996

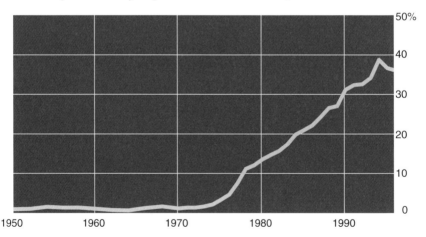

NOTE: Data for odd years from 1951 to 1969 are not available.

SOURCE: U.S. Department of Education, National Center for Education Statistics, "Degrees and Other Formal Awards Conferred" surveys, and Integrated Postsecondary Education Data System, "Completions" surveys.

FIGURE 2-13

Percentage of Medical Degrees Awarded to Women, 1950–1996

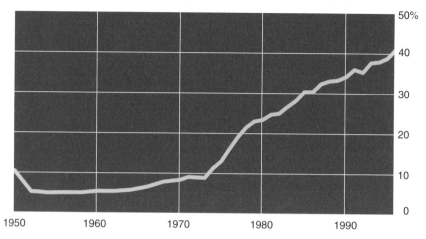

NOTE: Data for odd years from 1951 to 1969 are not available.

SOURCE: U.S. Department of Education, National Center for Education Statistics, "Degrees and Other Formal Awards Conferred" surveys, and Integrated Postsecondary Education Data System, "Completions" surveys.

Labor Force Participation

The labor force participation rate refers to the proportion of the population that is either employed or seeking to be employed. Outside the labor market are homemakers, retirees, the chronically ill, and others who simply are not seeking employment. The higher educational attainment of women is related to increased participation in the U.S. labor market, because increased labor market opportunities also encourage women to pursue further education. As figure 2-14 shows, female labor force participation increased from 26 percent in 1940 to 60 percent in 1997. Moreover, in the 1990s, more than 70 percent of women between the ages of twenty and fifty-four have been in the labor force. Working in the market economy rather than in the home has shifted from being the exception to being the norm for American women.

The U.S. labor market attracts and accommodates an increasingly educated and skilled women's work force. In 1952 nearly half the women in the labor market had less than a high school education. By 1998, as shown in figure 2-15, fewer than 9 percent of women in the work force had less than a high school education, and almost 60 percent of the women in the labor market had attended at least one year of college. While dramatic, the change in the educational attainment of women in the labor force over the past few decades differs little from the change for men. Studies do, however, show that the returns to education for women are higher than for men.[26] Men without high school or college degrees can get risky, high-paying jobs that involve substantial physical strength, whereas women are less likely to take such jobs. Hence, the difference between wages of educated and less-educated men is not so great as between educated and less-educated women. Consequently, the increased labor force participation rate of women over the same time period reflects changes in education as well as social and technological factors.

The number of women in the U.S. labor force has grown much more rapidly in the past fifty years than has the number of men. In 1997 women represented 46 percent of the labor force, as illustrated in figure 2-16. As figure 2-17 shows, the total number of women in the

FIGURE 2-14

Percentage of Adult Women Who Work, 1940–1997

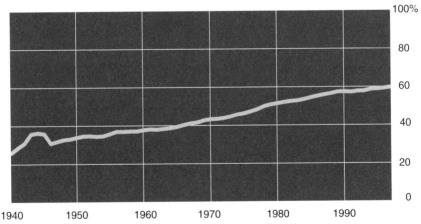

SOURCES: *Handbook of Labor Statistics,* 1988, table 5; *Historical Statistics,* vol. 1, series A, pp. 119–34, series D, pp. 29–41; *Statistical Abstract:* 1988, no. 625; 1993, no. 622; 1994, no. 615; and *Employment and Earnings,* vols. 43–45, no. 1, annual averages, table 3.

FIGURE 2-15

Distribution of Female Labor Force by Educational Attainment, 1952–1998

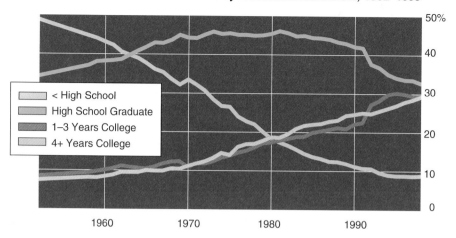

NOTE: Data for 1953–1956, 1958, 1960–1961, and 1963 are not available.

SOURCES: *Statistical Abstract:* 1991, no. 634; 1994, no. 617; *Handbook of Labor Statistics:* 1967, table 8; 1985, table 61; 1989, table 65; Bureau of Labor Statistics, unpublished data from the *Current Population Survey,* annual averages, 1992, 1993, 1994, 1995, 1996, 1997, and 1998.

FIGURE 2-16

Percentage of Labor Force That Is Women, 1948–1998

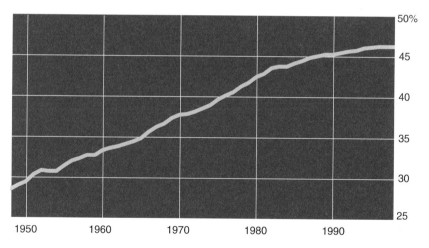

NOTE: Data for 1994–1996 are not strictly comparable with prior years owing to the introduction of a redesigned *Current Population Survey* questionnaire. Beginning in 1997, data are not strictly comparable with prior years because of revisions in the population controls used in the household survey.

SOURCE: U.S. Department of Labor, Bureau of Labor Statistics.

work force grew by more than 250 percent between 1948 and 1998. In contrast, the number of men in the labor force grew by only 70 percent during the same period. Figures 2-18 and 2-19 show that women's employment has more than doubled since 1968 in both full-time and part-time labor markets, with about a quarter of employed women working part-time. Thus, the increased employment is not an artifact of increased use of part-time employees.

Many researchers have suggested that technological changes have made household management and maintenance less time-consuming and have thus enabled millions engaged in household activities, primarily women, to enter the market labor force and to work more hours. According to a study of how Americans use their time, the amount women devote to housework has declined substantially: Women spent twenty-seven hours a week doing housework in 1965 but devoted only twenty-one hours a week to household chores in 1975 and nineteen hours a week in 1985.[27]

FIGURE 2-17

Total Employment by Sex, 1948–1998

(millions of workers)

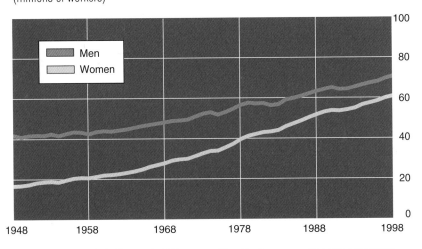

NOTE: Data for 1994–1996 are not strictly comparable with prior years owing to the introduction of a redesigned *Current Population Survey* questionnaire. Beginning in 1997, data are not strictly comparable with prior years because of revisions in the population controls used in the household survey.

SOURCE: U.S. Department of Labor, Bureau of Labor Statistics.

FIGURE 2-18

Full-Time Employment by Sex, 1968–1997

(millions of workers)

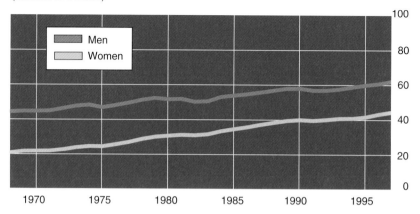

NOTE: Data for 1994–1996 are not strictly comparable with prior years owing to the introduction of a redesigned *Current Population Survey* questionnaire. Beginning in 1997, data reflect revised population controls used in the household survey.

SOURCES: U.S. Bureau of the Census, *Current Population Survey;* U.S. Department of Labor, Bureau of Labor Statistics, *Employment and Earnings.*

FIGURE 2-19

Part-Time Employment by Sex, 1968–1997

(millions of workers)

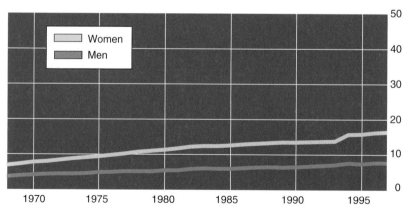

NOTE: Data for 1994–1996 are not strictly comparable with prior years owing to the introduction of a redesigned *Current Population Survey* questionnaire. Beginning in 1997, data reflect revised population controls used in the household survey.

SOURCES: U.S. Bureau of the Census, *Current Population Survey;* U.S. Department of Labor, Bureau of Labor Statistics, *Employment and Earnings.*

The greatest increase in women's labor force participation has occurred among married women. In 1920 only 9 percent of married women were in the labor force, and, as late as 1950, fewer than 25 percent of married women participated. As figure 2-20 shows, that number had risen to more than 60 percent by 1997. Increased employment among married women has not left families unaffected. What about the often-touted goal of having both career and family? As mentioned above, a study by Professor Claudia Goldin found that of women questioned who received college degrees around 1972 only about 15 percent were maintaining both career and family. Among those who have had a successful career, as indicated by income level, nearly 50 percent were childless. But college-educated women graduating between 1980 and 1995 are uncomfortable with the choice of "career then family" and intend to pursue both at the same point.[28]

FIGURE 2-20

Percentage of Women in the Labor Force by Marital Status, 1947–1997

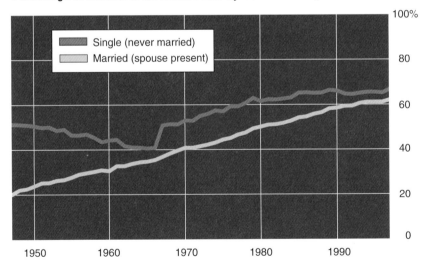

NOTES: Data for 1947–1966 include women fourteen years old and older. Beginning in 1967, all data refer to women ages sixteen and older. Single teenagers not in the labor force may be in school.

SOURCES: U.S. Department of Labor, Bureau of Labor Statistics, unpublished tabulations from the *Current Population Survey; Statistical Abstract,* 1995, no. 637.

Occupational Choice and the Pink Ghetto

While some feminists have made the glass ceiling a common rallying cry, they have also dominated the debate about occupational segregation. They believe that a "pink ghetto" limits women's workplace opportunities. The use of the word *ghetto*, with its connotations of powerlessness and hopelessness, is intentional. Those feminists claim that statistics reveal a very serious problem—women confined to low-paying jobs, presumably because of discrimination. In addition, such female-dominated occupations are alleged to pay significantly less than male-dominated occupations.

Central to the claims of a ghetto is the idea that a discriminatory society is limiting women's choices. Women do not choose certain careers on the basis of their personal preferences, qualifications, and future plans; instead, they are *funneled* into low-paying, low-status jobs. The switch to the passive voice in this debate is noteworthy, for the assumption is that women have not freely made those choices. Even when it is conceded that an element of choice was involved in a woman's decision to pursue a certain career, women are still thought to be in intolerable situations. Deborah Rhode argued that women are "trapped in part-time positions."[29] The Glass Ceiling Commission concluded that women were "locked into low wage, low prestige, and dead-end jobs."[30]

As Professor of Law Kingsley Browne noted, however, "On average, jobs held by women are rated as slightly higher in status than jobs held by men, because although men hold the highest-status jobs, they also hold the lowest ones." Men, Browne said, also have a "virtual monopoly" on the least attractive jobs.[31] Twenty-three of the twenty-five worst jobs as rated in *The Jobs Rated Almanac* are more than 90 percent male.[32]

We can perhaps best illustrate that by examining statistics on death rates on the job. According to Labor Department statistics, although 54 percent of the workplace is male, men account for 92 percent of all job-related deaths.[33] For every woman who dies on the job, thirteen men die. Some critics of existing occupational segregation patterns would respond by saying that no one forces men to take high-risk jobs, and they are often paid higher wages to perform them. But by that logic, no one forces women to accept lower-paying jobs in the pink ghettoes either.

Still, Eleanor Smeal of the Fund for the Feminist Majority, Mary Becker of the University of Chicago, and others note that some occupations still have fewer than 10 percent of female workers, and they cite that as evidence that discrimination persists and that affirmative action is still needed. Table 2-1 shows some of those occupations, which include mining, timber logging, construction, firefighting, and welding and cutting. Many of those jobs call for substantial amounts of physical strength and are hazardous. Some jobs such as truck driving also call for odd hours of work. Railroad transportation, as well as having unusual hours, is also a declining industry. A good case can be made that the low number of women in those lower-paying, high-risk trades is due to choice rather than discrimination.

In both cases, rational men and women have made individual choices; they have weighed the benefits and risks of a given job and have made a decision that is presumably in their best interest. Yet, for those who believe in systematic discrimination, one set of statistics, death rates on the job, is simply a workplace fact, while another set, those that reveal occupational segregation, is a problem that society created.

TABLE 2-1

Selected Occupations Less than 10 Percent Female, 1998

Occupation	% Female	Occupation	% Female
Airplane pilot or navigator	3.4	Pest controller	4.1
Construction laborer	4.5	Plant or systems operator	2.6
Construction trade worker	2.0	Precision metalworker	6.6
Extractive industry worker	1.4	Rail transport worker	5.1
Firefighter or fire preventor	2.5	Timber cutter or logger	3.0
Helper, construction or extractive	3.5	Truck driver	5.3
Material moving equipment operator	6.2	Welder or cutter	5.1
Mechanic or repairer	4.0		

SOURCE: U.S. Department of Labor, *Employment and Earnings*, table 11, January 1999.

The steady entrance of women into previously male-dominated educational programs has resulted in greater numbers of women entering and succeeding in traditionally male-dominated professions. Table 2-2 looks at the percentage of women in various professions in 1970 and 1998. Women represented about 12 percent of pharmacists in 1970 and nearly half in 1998. Between 1970 and 1998, women's representation increased from 5 to 29 percent of lawyers, from 27 to 66 percent of public relations specialists, and from 39 to 62 percent of psychologists. Other traditionally male-dominated areas have shown similar growth in numbers of female professionals.

But some observers see those results only as further evidence that women are victims of discrimination in the labor market. Most women, they argue, will never even have the opportunity to reach the business world because they are deliberately segregated into lower-paying jobs in the labor market. Such "occupational segregation" supposedly prevents women from entering higher-paying fields.

TABLE 2-2

Percentage of Women in Selected Occupations, 1970 and 1998

Occupation	1970	1998	Occupation	1970	1998
Architect	4	18	Pharmacist	12	44
Chemist, except biochemist	12	33	Physician	10	27
Cleric	3	12	Psychologist	39	62
Computer systems analyst			Public relations specialist	27	66
or scientist	14	27	Registered nurse	97	93
Dentist	4	20	Social worker	63	68
Dietician	92	86	Teacher		
Editor or reporter	42	51	Prekindergarten		
Engineer	2	11	or kindergarten	98	98
Lawyer	5	29	Elementary school	84	84
Librarian	82	83	Secondary school	50	57
Operations or systems			College or university	29	42
researcher or analyst	11	42			

SOURCES: Francine Blau and Marianne A. Ferber, *The Economics of Men, Women, and Work*, 2d ed. (Englewood Cliffs, N.J.: Prentice-Hall, 1992), table 5.3; U.S. Department of Labor, *Employment and Earnings,* table 11, January 1999.

A standard definition of *occupational segregation*, according to Andrea H. Beller in the *Journal of Human Resources,* is that "if more than half the population is denied access to 60 percent of the occupations, being crowded into a few at lower earnings, equality of opportunity does not exist."[34] Beller notes that "if women freely choose to enter only a third of all occupations and those occupations pay less, then women's lower earnings may not be a fundamental social problem."[35] The primary issue centers on the choices men and women have made in the labor market. Do those differences in occupational distributions occur because of personal choices made in an environment of equal opportunity or, as those who tout women's victimhood claim, in an environment of unequal opportunity and limited choice? In other words, is it plausible to claim that women working in "women's professions" or the "pink ghetto" have freely chosen to be there?

As Professor June O'Neill has pointed out, "Although pay in [typically] women's occupations has been found to be lower than pay in typically male occupations, this fact alone is not evidence of employer discrimination."[36] Many factors contribute to the concentration of women in certain professions, but one of the most important and overlooked is that many "pink-collar" jobs offer much-desired flexibility for working women. Many women are willing to accept substantially lower earnings to have a job with flexible hours.[37] Furthermore, many traditional female jobs require job skills that deteriorate slowly, allowing women to leave the work force for a time—to have children, for example—and still retain the skills needed to be viable job candidates when they return to the work force. In a field such as engineering, however, where job skills deteriorate rapidly, that would not be possible. Over time, occupational segregation has diminished and will continue to diminish. Women continue to enter and succeed in "male-dominated" professions, a trend that is the result of women's increased presence in certain "male" programs of higher education.

The pink ghetto is hardly the dead end that affirmative action supporters claim. The Glass Ceiling Commission conceded, for example, that the top two economic sectors expected to grow considerably between now and the year 2005 are female-dominated, namely, service/trade/retail and finance/insurance/real estate. In the years to come, the "ghetto" is likely to be an oasis for many women.

Women in Business

In addition to the outstanding gains women made in the professions, women are succeeding in the small-business world. Despite arguments about rampant discrimination and lack of opportunities, women nationwide have been starting their own businesses and succeeding. One reason for that could be that the increased flexibility of self-employment benefits women and motivates success.

Today, over 8.5 million women-owned businesses in the United States employ 23.8 million people and generate $3.1 trillion in revenue. The number of women-owned businesses more than doubled from 1987 to 1997.[38] According to a study by the National Foundation of Women Business Owners, women are starting businesses at twice the rate of men.[39] Figure 2-21 shows the increase in the number of women-owned businesses from 1972 to 1997.

What are some characteristics of these women-owned businesses? Figure 2-22 shows that women-owned businesses are found in all industries. The majority are in the service sector, accounting for 52 per-

FIGURE 2-21

Number of Women-Owned Businesses, 1972–1997

(millions)

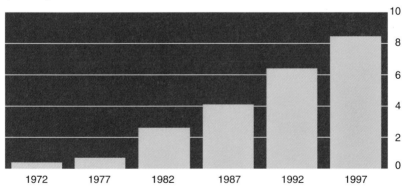

NOTE: Data for 1992 and 1997 include C corporations.

SOURCES: U.S. Bureau of the Census, *Economic Census,* "Women-Owned Businesses," 1977, table 1; 1987, table 1. U.S. Small Business Administration, Office of Advocacy, *Women in Business,* October 1998, table 1, 1992 and 1997.

cent, followed by retail trade, with 19 percent, followed by finance, insurance, and real estate, with 10 percent. Women are progressing in other industries: many new women-owned small businesses are in construction, wholesale trade, transportation, and agribusiness.

Over the past nine years, the states with the highest growth rates of women-owned businesses have been Nevada (130 percent), Georgia (112 percent), New Mexico (108 percent), Florida (106 percent), and Idaho (104 percent). The state with the slowest growth has been New Mexico, with a growth rate of 40 percent.

Women are also starting home-based businesses in record numbers. Data show that women own about 37 percent of the more than 9 million home-based businesses, or about 3.5 million such businesses, according to data from the U.S. Census Bureau.[40] The latest census, in 1992, showed that more than 60 percent of women-owned businesses were started in a home, and 58 percent were still in that home in 1992.

The Small Business Administration estimates that "by the year 2000, women-owned sole proprietorships will number 7.1 million or 35 percent of U.S. sole proprietorships,"[41] which will be an 8 percent increase from 1990. Such statistics suggest that women do not face an economy saturated with sex discrimination.

FIGURE 2-22

Industry Distribution of Women-Owned Firms, 1996

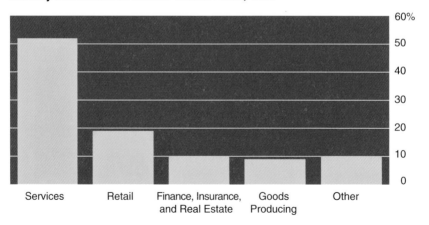

NOTE: Goods-producing industries are defined as agriculture, manufacturing, and construction.

SOURCE: National Foundation for Women Business Owners, "Facts on Women-Owned Businesses, State Trends," 1996.

Elected Officials

Business is not the only realm in which women are exercising greater influence. They are also entering the political arena, competing for—and winning—elective office. In 1998 the top five government officials elected to office in Arizona—governor, secretary of state, treasurer, attorney general, and superintendent of public instruction—were women. Deborah Walsh of the Center for the American Woman and Politics (CAWP) commented, "It's a pretty big deal. We've never seen this before. It's really the culmination of 30 years in American politics, and with luck, we'll start seeing more of this."[42]

Tables 2-3 and 2-4 show the increasing tendency of women in recent years to run in one of the two major political parties for both the U.S. Congress and selected state offices. In 1974, for example, 47 women were candidates of one of the major political parties for

TABLE 2-3

Summary of Women Candidates for U.S. Congressional Offices, 1968–1998

Election Year	Senate		House	
1968	1	(1D, 0R)	19	(12D, 7R)
1970	1	(0D, 1R)	25	(15D, 10R)
1972	2	(0D, 2R)	32	(24D, 8R)
1974	3	(2D, 1R)	44	(30D, 14R)
1976	1	(1D, 0R)	54	(34D, 20R)
1978	2	(1D, 1R)	46	(27D, 19R)
1980	5	(2D, 3R)	52	(27D, 25R)
1982	3	(1D, 2R)	55	(27D, 28R)
1984	10	(6D, 4R)	65	(30D, 35R)
1986	6	(3D, 3R)	64	(30D, 34R)
1988	2	(0D, 2R)	59	(33D, 26R)
1990	8	(2D, 6R)	69	(39D, 30R)
1992	11	(10D, 1R)	106	(70D, 36R)
1994	9	(4D, 5R)	112	(72D, 40R)
1996	9	(5D, 4R)	120	(77D, 42R, 1I)
1998	10	(7D, 3R)	121	(75D, 46R)

NOTES: Data include minor party candidates only if their parties have recently won statewide offices. Data since 1990 do not include the delegates from Washington, D.C., and the five territories.

SOURCE: Center for the American Woman and Politics, Eagleton Institute of Politics, Rutgers University.

TABLE 2-4

Summary of Women Candidates for State Executive and Legislative Offices, 1974–1998

Election Year	Governor	Lt. Governor	Secretary of State	State Auditor	State Treasurer	State Legislator
1974	3 (1D, 2R)	4 (1D, 3R)	14 (6D, 8R)	5 (3D, 2R)	10 (8D, 2R)	1,125
1976	2 (2D, 0R)	1 (0D, 1R)	3 (0D, 3R)	0	6 (3D, 3R)	1,258
1978	1 (1D, 0R)	9 (6D, 3R)	16 (9D, 7R)	2 (2D, 0R)	10 (6D, 4R)	1,348
1980	0	3 (2D, 1R)	4 (1D, 3R)	3 (2D, 1R)	3 (2D, 1R)	1,426
1982	2 (2D, 0R)	7 (4D, 3R)	14 (7D, 7R)	1 (1D, 0R)	10 (6D, 4R)	1,643
1984	1 (1D, 0R)	6 (4D, 2R)	6 (4D, 2R)	4 (2D, 2R)	1 (1D, 0R)	1,756
1986	8 (3D, 5R)	11 (6D, 5R)	21 (14D, 7R)	6 (4D, 2R)	11 (7D, 4R)	1,813
1988	2 (2D, 0R)	2 (1D, 1R)	3 (2D, 1R)	2 (0D, 2R)	2 (1D, 1R)	1,853
1990	8 (4D, 4R)	19 (8D, 10R, 1I)	17 (8D, 9R)	7 (5D, 2R)	16 (8D, 8R)	2,064
1992	3 (2D, 1R)	7 (3D, 4R)	5 (3D, 2R)	1 (0D, 1R)	5 (3D, 2R)	2,375
1994	10 (6D, 3R, 1I)	29 (14D, 13R, 2I)	20 (8D, 12R)	4 (1D, 3R)	16 (11D, 5R)	2,284
1996	6 (3R, 3D)	9 (5D, 4R)	4 (4D, 0R)	2 (2D, 0R)	7 (3D, 4R)	2,274
1998	21 (14D, 7R)	42 (22D, 20R)	32 (18D, 14R)	9 (5D, 4R)	18 (8D, 9R, 1I)	2,279

NOTES: Data include minor party candidates only if their parties have recently won statewide offices. Data since 1990 do not include the delegates from Washington, D.C., and the five territories.

SOURCE: Center for the American Woman and Politics, Eagleton Institute of Politics, Rutgers University.

Congress; 36 women were candidates for state executive offices; and 1,125 women were candidates for state legislatures. In 1998 more than twice as many women were running for Congress (131) and for state legislatures (2,279); and more than three times as many (122) were running for statewide office. Figure 2-23 shows the increase in numbers of female congressional candidates from 1968 to 1998.

A 1997 study by Jody Newman of the National Women's Political Caucus found negligible differences between men and women in success rates in winning state and national races. The main reason more women are not in office is not that women do not win, but that they do not run. In total, the study found no evidence that women had fewer chances to win than men.[43] That is not a minor point. Claims of societywide discrimination against women sound increasingly more hollow when the data show that voting members of that society choose female candidates as often as they choose male candidates. Those sim-

FIGURE 2-23

Number of Women Candidates for U.S. Congressional Offices, 1968–1998

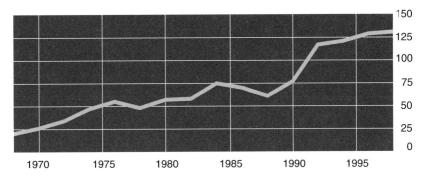

NOTES: Data include minor party candidates only if their parties have recently won statewide offices. Data after 1990 do not include the delegates from Washington, D.C., and the five territories.

SOURCE: Center for the American Woman and Politics, Eagleton Institute of Politics, Rutgers University.

FIGURE 2-24

Number of Women in the U.S. Congress, 1917–1999

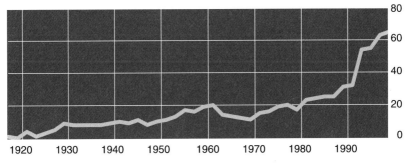

NOTES: Table shows maximum number of women elected or appointed to serve in that Congress at one time period. Some filled out unexpired terms, and some were never sworn in.

SOURCE: Center for the American Woman and Politics, Eagleton Institute of Politics, Rutgers University.

ilar success rates suggest that what matters are issues and a candidate's ability to tackle them, regardless of sex. Women are likely to continue to enter the political arena and represent the full range of perspectives and philosophies.

Figure 2-24 and table 2-5 show the number of women in Congress since the 65th Congress in 1917. Until 1981, no more than

TABLE 2-5

Summary of Women in the U.S. Congress, 1917–2001

Congress	Term Years	Senate	House	Total
65th	1917–1919	0 (0D, 0R)	1 (0D, 1R)	1 (0D, 1R)
66th	1919–1921	0 (0D, 0R)	0 (0D, 0R)	0 (0D, 0R)
67th	1921–1923	1 (1D, 0R)	3 (0D, 3R)	4 (1D, 3R)
68th	1923–1925	0 (0D, 0R)	1 (0D, 1R)	1 (0D, 1R)
69th	1925–1927	0 (0D, 0R)	3 (1D, 2R)	3 (1D, 2R)
70th	1927–1929	0 (0D, 0R)	5 (2D, 3R)	5 (2D, 3R)
71st	1929–1931	0 (0D, 0R)	9 (5D, 4R)	9 (5D, 4R)
72d	1931–1933	1 (1D, 0R)	7 (5D, 2R)	8 (6D, 2R)
73d	1933–1935	1 (1D, 0R)	7 (4D, 3R)	8 (5D, 3R)
74th	1935–1937	2 (2D, 0R)	6 (4D, 2R)	8 (6D, 2R)
75th	1937–1939	2 (1D, 1R)	6 (5D, 1R)	8 (6D, 2R)
76th	1939–1941	1 (1D, 0R)	8 (4D, 4R)	9 (5D, 4R)
77th	1941–1943	1 (1D, 0R)	9 (4D, 5R)	10 (5D, 5R)
78th	1943–1945	1 (1D, 0R)	8 (2D, 6R)	9 (3D, 6R)
79th	1945–1947	0 (0D, 0R)	11 (6D, 5R)	11 (6D, 5R)
80th	1947–1949	1 (0D, 1R)	7 (3D, 4R)	8 (3D, 5R)
81st	1949–1951	1 (0D, 1R)	9 (5D, 4R)	10 (5D, 5R)
82d	1951–1953	1 (0D, 1R)	10 (4D, 6R)	11 (4D, 7R)
83d	1953–1955	2 (0D, 2R)	11 (5D, 6R)	13 (5D, 8R)
84th	1955–1957	1 (0D, 1R)	16 (10D, 6R)	17 (10D, 7R)
85th	1957–1959	1 (0D, 1R)	15 (9D, 6R)	16 (9D, 7R)
86th	1959–1961	2 (1D, 1R)	17 (9D, 8R)	19 (10D, 9R)
87th	1961–1963	2 (1D, 1R)	18 (11D, 7R)	20 (12D, 8R)
88th	1963–1965	2 (1D, 1R)	12 (6D, 6R)	14 (7D, 7R)
89th	1965–1967	2 (1D, 1R)	11 (7D, 4R)	13 (8D, 5R)
90th	1967–1969	1 (0D, 1R)	11 (6D, 5R)	12 (6D, 6R)
91st	1969–1971	1 (0D, 1R)	10 (6D, 4R)	11 (6D, 5R)
92d	1971–1973	2 (1D, 1R)	13 (10D, 3R)	15 (11D, 4R)
93d	1973–1975	0 (0D, 0R)	16 (14D, 2R)	16 (14D, 2R)
94th	1975–1977	0 (0D, 0R)	19 (14D, 5R)	19 (14D, 5R)
95th	1977–1979	2 (2D, 0R)	18 (13D, 5R)	20 (15D, 5R)
96th	1979–1981	1 (0D, 1R)	16 (11D, 5R)	17 (11D, 6R)
97th	1981–1983	2 (0D, 2R)	21 (11D, 10R)	23 (11D, 12R)
98th	1983–1985	2 (0D, 2R)	22 (13D, 9R)	24 (13D, 11R)
99th	1985–1987	2 (0D, 2R)	23 (12D, 11R)	25 (12D, 13R)
100th	1987–1989	2 (1D, 1R)	23 (12D, 11R)	25 (13D, 12R)
101st	1989–1991	2 (1D, 1R)	29 (16D, 13R)	31 (17D, 14R)
102d	1991–1993	4 (3D, 1R)	28 (19D, 9R)	32 (22D, 10R)
103d	1993–1995	7 (5D, 2R)	47 (35D, 12R)	54 (40D, 14R)
104th	1995–1997	9 (5D, 4R)	48 (31D, 17R)	57 (36D, 21R)
105th	1997–1999	9 (6D, 3R)	54 (37D, 17R)	63 (43D, 20R)
106th	1999–2001	9 (6D, 3R)	56 (39D, 17R)	65 (45D, 20R)

NOTES: Table shows maximum number of women elected or appointed to serve in that Congress at one time period. Some filled out unexpired terms, and some were never sworn in.

SOURCE: Center for the American Woman and Politics, Eagleton Institute of Politics, Rutgers University.

twenty women had served in Congress at one time. Today, 9 of 100 senators and 56 of 435 representatives are women. Although the number of elected women government officials remains small relative to men, the increasing numbers do reveal a gradual acceptance of women's place in national government. Women have also been increasing their numbers in state legislatures and in state executive offices. According to CAWP, in 1999 22.3 percent of state legislators are women, compared with 4 percent in 1969. Women represented 27.6 percent of statewide elective officials. CAWP reported 1,427 female winners in state legislative races in 1998.

Voting Patterns

In recent years the media have emphasized the "gender gap" in voting, suggesting that women as a group vote in greater numbers for Democratic candidates than for Republican candidates. According to public opinion analyst Karlyn Bowman,

> The difference in political preferences of male and female voters is only one of many gaps in voting preferences in U.S. politics. In the 1998 election, for example, 46 percent of men voted for Democratic congressional candidates and 54 percent for Republicans. Fifty-three percent of women voted for Democrats, and 47 percent for Republicans. The gender gap was fourteen percentage points.[44]

Bowman also noted:

> A gap in the preferences of married and nonmarried voters was present in 1998, too, just as it has been in past elections. Forty-four percent of married voters pulled the lever for Democratic congressional candidates and 56 percent for Republican ones. By contrast, 60 percent of voters who indicated they were not married voted for Democratic congressional candidates and 40 percent for GOP ones, so the marriage gap was thirty-two points.[45]

The 1998 Election Day exit polls performed by the Voter News Service reveal substantial differences in the voting patterns of

African American and white women. A majority of African American women voted for Democrats in the November elections. In contrast, a majority of white women voted for Republicans.[46] Domesticity tends to turn white women, but not African American women, toward voting Republican. According to Kellyanne Fitzpatrick, president of the Polling Company, "[T]he three Ms— marriage, mortgages, and munchkins—cause white women to vote for Republicans."[47]

Women have been voting at a steadily increasing rate for decades, finally matching the male voting rate in the 1980 elections. Since then, women have been voting in greater numbers than men, especially in national elections. Tables 2-6 and 2-7 present the small differences between the percentage of eligible men and women voting in presidential and nonpresidential elections, respectively. Notice, however, that because women account for a larger portion of adult Americans, equal percentages of eligible women voting translate into greater *numbers* of women than men voting in U.S. elections.

TABLE 2-6

Differences in Voter Turnout for Presidential Elections by Sex, 1964–1996

Election Year	% Voting Age Population Who Reported Voting		Number Who Reported Voting (millions)	
	Women	Men	Women	Men
1964	67.0	71.9	39.2	37.5
1968	66.0	69.8	41.0	38.0
1972	62.0	64.1	44.9	40.9
1976	58.8	59.6	45.6	41.1
1980	59.4	59.1	49.3	43.8
1984	60.8	59.0	54.5	47.4
1988	58.3	56.4	54.5	47.7
1992	62.3	60.2	60.6	53.3
1996	55.5	52.8	56.1	48.9

SOURCE: Center for the American Woman and Politics, Eagleton Institute of Politics, Rutgers University.

TABLE 2-7

Differences in Voter Turnout for Nonpresidential Elections by Sex, 1966–1994

Election Year	% Voting Age Population Who Reported Voting		Number Who Reported Voting (millions)	
	Women	Men	Women	Men
1966	53.0	58.2	31.8	30.7
1970	52.7	56.8	33.8	32.0
1974	43.4	46.2	32.5	30.7
1978	45.3	46.6	36.3	33.3
1982	48.4	48.7	42.3	38.0
1986	46.1	45.8	42.2	37.7
1990	45.4	44.6	43.3	38.7
1994	44.9	44.4	44.6	40.4

Source: Center for the American Woman and Politics, Eagleton Institute of Politics, Rutgers University.

NOTES

1. U.S. Department of Labor, Bureau of Labor Statistics, unpublished tables.

2. Sharon M. Oster, "Is There a Policy Problem? The Gender Wage Gap," *Georgetown Law Journal*, vol. 82 (1993), pp. 109–19.

3. U.S. Bureau of the Census, *Current Population Reports*, Series P-20-482 (Washington, D.C.: Government Printing Office, 1995).

4. Catalyst, *The 1998 Catalyst Census of Women Corporate Officers and Top Earners* (New York: Catalyst, November 1998).

5. Institute for Women's Policy Research, *The Status of Women in the States, Second Edition, 1998–1999* (Washington, D.C.: Institute for Women's Policy Research, October 1998).

6. David Macpherson and Barry Hirsch, "Wages and Gender Composition: Why Do Women's Jobs Pay Less?" *Journal of Labor Economics*, vol. 13 (1995), pp. 426–71.

7. June O'Neill, "The Shrinking Pay Gap," *Wall Street Journal*, October 7, 1994, p. A10.

8. Ibid.

9. Jane Waldfogel, "Working Mothers Then and Now: A Cross-Cohort Analysis of the Effects of Maternity Leave on Women's Pay," in Francine D. Blau and Ronald G. Ehrenberg, eds., *Gender and Family Issues in the Workplace* (New York: Russell Sage Foundation, 1997).

10. See, for example, Sanders Korenman and David Neumark, "Marriage, Motherhood, and Wages," *Journal of Human Resources*, vol. 27 (1992), pp. 233–55; David Neumark and Sanders Korenman, "Sources of Bias in Women's Wage Equations: Results Using Sibling Data," *Journal of Human Resources,* vol. 29 (1994), pp. 379–405.

11. Claudia Goldin, "Career and Family: College Women Look to the Past," in Francine Blau and Ronald Ehrenberg, eds., *Gender and Family Issues in the Workplace* (New York: Russell Sage Foundation, 1997).

12. Chinhui Juhn and Kevin Murphy, "Wage Inequality and Family Labor Supply," *Journal of Labor Economics,* vol. 15 (1997), pp. 72–97.

13. Jacob Mincer, "Labor Force Participation of Married Women: A Study of Labor Supply," in C. Christ, ed., *Aspects of Labor Economics* (Princeton: Princeton University Press, 1962).

14. Suzanne Nossel and Elizabeth Westfall, *Presumed Equal: What America's Top Women Lawyers Really Think about Their Firms* (Franklin Lakes, N.J.: Career Press, 1998), p. xvii.

15. Ibid., p. xviii.

16. Ibid., p. xix.

17. Ibid., p. xx.

18. Ibid., p. xxii.

19. Elizabeth Fox-Genovese, *Feminism Is Not the Story of My Life* (New York: Doubleday, 1996).

20. Glass Ceiling Commission, *Good for Business: Making Full Use of the Nation's Human Capital* (Washington, D.C.: Government Printing Office, March 1995), p. 143.

21. Korn/Ferry, *Korn/Ferry International's 25th Annual Board of Directors Study* (New York: Korn/Ferry, April 1998).

22. Glass Ceiling Commission, *Good for Business,* p. 28.

23. Michael Lynch and Katherine Post, "What Glass Ceiling?" *The Public Interest,* no. 124 (Summer 1996), pp. 27–36.

24. During World War II, the percentage of graduates who were women increased because most university-aged men were in the armed services.

25. U.S. Department of Education, Integrated Postsecondary Education Data System, "Completions" survey, 1996; *Digest of Education Statistics, 1997* (Washington, D.C.: Government Printing Office, 1997), table 188.

26. Marvin Kosters, *Wage Levels and Inequality: Measuring and Interpreting the Trends* (Washington, D.C.: AEI Press, 1998).

27. John Robinson and Geoffrey Godbey, *Time for Life: The Surprising Ways Americans Use Their Time* (University Park, Penn.: Pennsylvania State University Press, 1997), table 3, p. 105.

28. Goldin, "Career and Family: College Women Look to the Past."

29. Deborah Rhode, *Speaking of Sex: The Denial of Gender Inequality* (Cambridge: Harvard University Press, 1997), p. 142.

30. Glass Ceiling Commission, *Good for Business*, p. 12.

31. Kingsley R. Browne, "Sex and Temperament in Modern Society: A Darwinian View of the Glass Ceiling and the Gender Gap." *Arizona Law Review*, vol. 37 (1995), pp. 971–1106.

32. Les Krantz, *The Jobs Rated Almanac*, rev. ed. (New York: World Almanac, 1992), p. 13.

33. U.S. Department of Labor, Bureau of Labor Statistics, *Census of Fatal Occupational Injuries, 1997* (Washington, D.C.: Government Printing Office, 1998), and U.S. Department of Labor, Bureau of Labor Statistics, *Survey of Occupational Injuries and Illnesses, 1996* (Washington, D.C.: Government Printing Office, 1998).

34. Andrea H. Beller, "Occupational Segregation by Sex: Determinants and Changes," *Journal of Human Resources*, vol. 17 (Summer 1982), pp. 371–92.

35. Ibid.

36. June O'Neill, "Comparable Worth," in David R. Henderson, ed., *Fortune Encyclopedia of Economics* (New York: Warner Books, 1993).

37. Wendy Lee Gramm, "Household Utility Maximization and the Working Wife," *American Economic Review*, vol. 65 (March 1975), pp. 90–100.

38. U.S. Small Business Administration, Office of Advocacy, *Women in Business* (Washington, D.C.: Government Printing Office, October 1998).

39. National Foundation of Women Business Owners, Catalyst, and The Committee of 200, *Paths to Entrepreneurship: New Directions for Women in Business* (February 1998).

40. U.S. Department of the Census, *Characteristics of Small Business Owners* (Washington, D.C.: Government Printing Office, 1992).

41. U.S. Small Business Administration, Office of Advocacy, *Women in Business*, p. 8.

42. As quoted in Valerie Richardson, "Women Take Over in Arizona; Will Enter State's Top Five Offices," *Washington Times*, December 30, 1998, pp. A1, A18.

43. Jody Newman, "The Gender Story: Women as Voters and Candidates in the 1996 Elections," in Regina Dougherty, Everett C. Ladd, David Wilber, and Lynn Zayachkiwsky, eds., *America at the Polls 1996* (Storrs, Conn.: Roper Center for Public Opinion Research, 1997), p. 106.

44. Conversation with Karlyn Bowman, resident fellow, American Enterprise Institute, January 4, 1999.

45. Ibid.

46. Marjorie Connelly, "A Look at Voting Patterns of 115 Demographic Groups in House Races," *New York Times*, November 9, 1998, p. A20. The 1998 data come from Voter News Service.

47. Presentation by Kellyanne Fitzpatrick, Polling Company, November 4, 1998.

PART
III

Women, Poverty, and the Government

*I*f men were systematically advantaged in American society, one might expect to find many economic and social indicia in which men are persistently and steadily better off than women. Although many indicators by which men remain ahead of women exist, the gap in most instances is shrinking, as we described above.

Statistics paint an ambiguous portrait of the differences between men and women in the areas of health and crime. Men, for example, are far less susceptible than women to certain health conditions such as osteoporosis. They are, however, statistically more likely than women to be victims of heart disease when under the age of sixty-five or the victims of murder. Women also live longer than men, as figure 3-1 shows. While those different outcomes in health statistics could, theoretically, be the result of discrimination in the allocation of federal funds for medical research or for crime prevention, it is unclear from the available evidence whether that is, in fact, the case.[1]

Measures of Poverty

The one area where women consistently suffer more than men, however, is poverty as measured by the federal government. Poverty disproportionately affects women in American society. Although women were 51.3 percent of the population in 1990, they accounted for 57.7 percent of all persons living in poverty. As figure 3-2 illustrates, between 1966 and 1997 female poverty rates consistently exceeded male rates by approximately three percentage points.[2] While absolute measures of poverty remain elusive and while government measures

FIGURE 3-1

Life Expectancy at Birth by Sex, 1920–1996

(age in years)

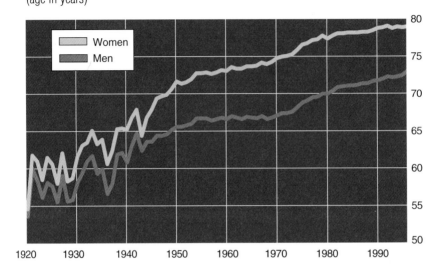

SOURCES: *Historical Statistics,* vol. 1, series B, pp.107–15; *Statistical Abstract,* 1998, no. 128; *Vital Statistics,* 1985, no. 102; *World Almanac,* 1998, p. 973.

FIGURE 3-2

Percentage of Population below Poverty Line by Sex, 1966–1997

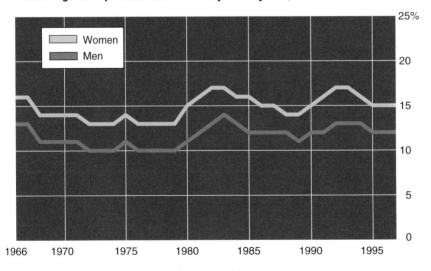

SOURCE: U.S. Bureau of the Census, *Current Population Survey.*

are often criticized, there is relatively little skepticism about the general finding of consistently greater incidence of poverty among women.

The statistics provide a number of clues about the life cycle of female poverty. For example, poverty rates for male and female children are almost equal. But between the ages of eighteen and twenty-four, women experience a 60 percent higher rate of poverty than men in the same age group. The rates differ significantly again among the elderly. The poverty rate among women over the age of sixty-five is twice the rate of men. Demographic evidence suggests that this "feminization of poverty" will most likely continue.

Can government programs successfully target those female-headed households in poverty? Many federal programs already target predominantly female single heads of households. Survivor benefits of government pension programs and Social Security primarily aid single, elderly women, and the majority of funding under the Temporary Assistance for Needy Families (TANF) block grant goes to working unmarried heads of households.

Demographic trends also contribute to difficulties in tackling problems like female poverty. People are living longer, and women are living much longer than men, as figure 3-1 shows. In 1920 male life expectancy was 53.6 years, and female life expectancy was 54.6 years. By 1996 the life expectancy at birth for men had risen to seventy-three years and for women to seventy-nine years. The differences in life expectancy between men and women in the United States do not reflect substantial differences in infant or child morbidity but rather significant differences in the death rates for middle-aged and elderly men and women. The net result is a large and growing population of households consisting of single, elderly women. The proportion of the population that is elderly is growing, and the population that is elderly, single, and female is growing even more rapidly.

Households headed by elderly unmarried women are more likely than many other types of households to be in poverty for several reasons. The elderly, male and female, have few employment options to earn income. Most definitions of poverty measure only income, which is relatively easy to observe, rather than consumption or wealth, both of which are more difficult to observe. Yet the income patterns of an elderly household may have little relationship with either the consumption or wealth patterns of that household.

Poverty by any measure can still be acute for the elderly, particularly for female-headed households. Elderly households often consume savings built up over a lifetime. For elderly married couples, wives are more likely to survive their husbands by several years both because of a greater life expectancy and because women tend to marry men older than themselves. As a result, retirement savings, which may have been adequate at the date of retirement, may dwindle in later years when the wife is more likely to be a single survivor.

Young women are also heading up one-person households in unprecedented numbers, partly as a result of other demographic trends. Women are postponing marriage, thus creating a large population of young, single women. Between 1947 and 1973, as shown in figure 3-3, the median age at first marriage for women never exceeded twenty-one years of age. Since 1973, the median age at first marriage for women has steadily increased, reaching twenty-five years of age in 1997. That trend is largely the result of women's new educational and career opportunities. Now that significant numbers of women are attending college and pursuing professional lives upon graduation, they have delayed marriage and childbearing.[3]

The rising incidence of divorce has also led to a much larger relative population of young single women. Figure 3-4 shows the increased incidence of divorce per 1,000 married women over the past few decades. Although divorce rates have plateaued since the mid-1970s, divorce is still much more common than in earlier decades. Figure 3-5 illustrates the distribution of American women age eighteen or older by marital status since 1950. In that year 20 percent of adult women were single and only 2 percent were divorced. By 1998 the percentage of single women grew only slightly to 21 percent, but the percentage of divorced women increased almost fivefold to 11 percent. Taken together, the postponed age of marriage and the high incidence of divorce have led to an increase in the relative population of young female-headed households, a considerable percentage of which are vulnerable to poverty.

Many female-headed households have children present either from earlier marriages or from the increased rate of illegitimate

FIGURE 3-3

Median Age at First Marriage by Sex, 1947–1998

(age in years)

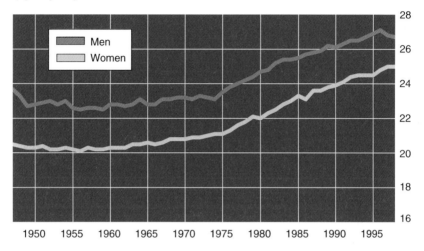

SOURCE: U.S. Bureau of the Census, *Current Population Reports,* series P20-514, "Marital Status and Living Arrangements: March 1998 (Update)," and earlier reports.

FIGURE 3-4

Divorce Rates per 1,000 Married Women, 1920–1997

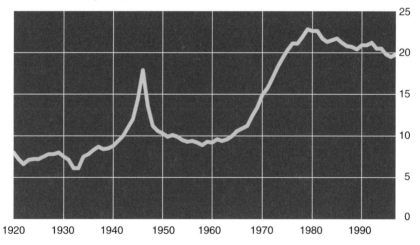

SOURCES: *Historical Statistics,* vol. 1, series B, pp. 216–20; *Vital Statistics:* 1971, pp. 2–6; *Statistical Abstract:* 1974, no. 93; 1978, no. 114; 1980, no. 124; 1982, no. 120; 1986, no. 124; 1991, no. 139; 1995, nos. 142 and 146; 1997, no. 145; National Center for Health Statistics, unpublished data.

FIGURE 3-5

Marital Status of Women, Percentage Distribution, 1950–1998

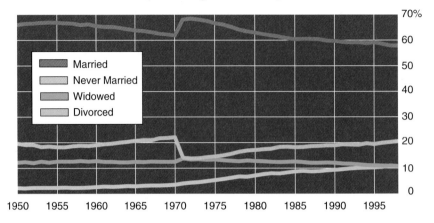

NOTES: Data for 1950–1970 include women fourteen years old or older. Data since 1971 include women eighteen years old or older.

SOURCES: *Statistical Abstract:* 1960, no. 36; 1962, no. 32; 1963, no. 31; 1964, no. 29; 1965, no. 29; 1966, no. 32; 1967, no. 32; 1969, no. 37; 1970, no. 36; 1971, no. 38; 1972, no. 46; 1980, no. 51; 1983, no. 44; 1989, no. 50; 1990, no. 50; 1991, no. 50; 1992, no. 49; 1993, no. 49; 1994, no. 59; 1995, no. 58; 1997, no. 58; 1998, no. 61; *Historical Statistics*, series A, pp. 160–71; U.S. Bureau of the Census, unpublished tabulation.

births. As shown in figure 3-6, the illegitimacy rate in the United States increased from slightly more than seven births per 1,000 unmarried women of childbearing age in 1940 to almost forty-five births per 1,000 unmarried women of childbearing age in 1996. Although the rate has declined from its peak of forty-seven births per 1,000 unmarried women in 1994, rates are still at historically high levels. At the same time, as shown in figure 3-7, the total birth rate declined from eighty births per 1,000 women of childbearing age in 1940 to sixty-five births per 1,000 women of childbearing age in 1996. The net result is that both the percentage of illegitimate births and the proportion of families headed by unmarried women increased dramatically. Figure 3-8 shows that the percentage of families with children headed by women has more than tripled from 6 percent in 1950 to 22 percent in 1998.

Even leaving aside the lower levels of social and educational achievement that are often associated with one-parent households,

FIGURE 3-6

Births per 1,000 Unmarried Women Ages 15–44, 1940–1996

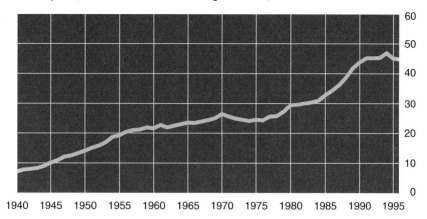

SOURCES: *Historical Statistics*, vol. 1, series B28-35, p. 52; *Vital Statistics:* 1972, pp. 1–30; *Statistical Abstract:* 1980, no. 95; 1987, no. 86; 1990, no. 90; 1992, no. 89; 1994, no. 100; 1995, no. 94. *Monthly Vital Statistics Report:* 1997, vol. 45, no. 11(s), table 15; 1998, vol. 46, no. 11(s), table 17; National Center for Health Statistics.

FIGURE 3-7

Births per 1,000 Women Ages 15–44, 1940–1996

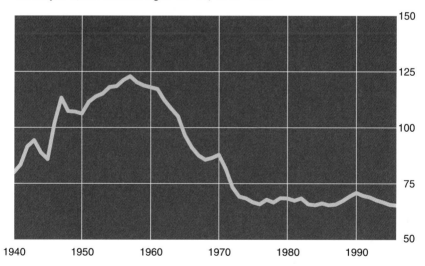

SOURCES: *Historical Statistics,* vol. 1, series B, pp. 20–27; *Statistical Abstract:* 1979, no. 83; 1980, no. 87; 1982, no. 84; 1985, no. 82; 1994, no. 92; 1995, no. 93; *Monthly Vital Statistics Report:* 1997, vol. 45, no. 11(s), table 10; 1998, vol. 46, no. 11(s), table 13; National Center for Health Statistics.

FIGURE 3-8

Percentage Distribution of Families with Children under 18 by Family Head, 1950–1998

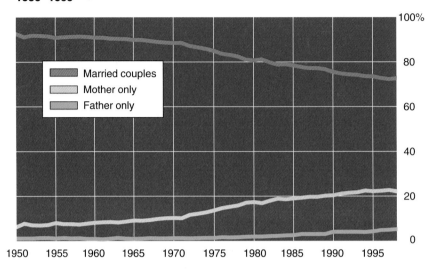

NOTE: Data for 1970 and 1980 include revisions from the Census Bureau.

SOURCE: U.S. Bureau of the Census, *Current Population Reports,* series P20-515, "Household and Family Characteristics: March 1998 (Update)," and earlier reports.

for several reasons families with children headed by an unmarried woman are more likely to live in poverty than is a family with two parents present. Family income for young families is based primarily on wage income rather than on income from accumulated capital. The opportunities for earned income are much greater with two earners than with one earner. More important, the choice of employment options is limited for the parent who bears most or all of the responsibility for child-rearing activities. The single parent is the only one who bears that responsibility and employment limitation. Those child-rearing activities consume time that could otherwise be spent earning income. Moreover, those activities make it difficult for a parent to accept employment with variable or uncertain hours, a characteristic of many jobs in the labor market. Unlike a one-parent family, the two-parent family can have both earners in the labor market, one of whom can accept a more highly compensated, variable-hour position.

Women and Welfare Reform

Poverty-prone, unmarried, female-headed households are not entirely the result of independent demographic trends; some government programs themselves have influenced the great incidence of young female-headed households and the poverty associated with them. The federally funded Aid to Families with Dependent Children (AFDC) program used to provide entitlements to unmarried women—but not men—with children in poverty. The economically rational decision for a young, unmarried couple with a child but with few resources and few prospects for employment was to have the mother and the child, but not the father, apply for AFDC benefits. The AFDC program created incentives for unmarried motherhood and disincentives for marriage and the enforcement of the parental responsibility of the father. Under the AFDC program, welfare caseloads increased to record highs.

In 1996, however, Congress approved the TANF program and abolished the AFDC program. The TANF program allowed states to design their own welfare programs, within certain parameters, and ended the federal entitlement to benefits.

The TANF program operates as follows. Each state receives a block grant, and funds can be spent on cash and noncash benefits, services, and administrative costs. In general, states are not allowed to help families in which an adult has received sixty months of benefits. Teenagers who receive benefits must go to school and live at home, and fathers must provide child support. Requirements exist for welfare recipients to work or engage in community service.

Even before the TANF program was implemented, welfare caseloads began a remarkable decline, and they have now fallen by approximately 40 percent. About 2 million fewer families, the majority of them headed by women, and 5 million fewer recipients received benefits in 1998 than in 1993. The growing economy and decreasing unemployment rate, reaching a low of 4.3 percent in 1998, also contributed to the decline in numbers of welfare recipients.

Professors Geoffrey Wallace and Rebecca Blank, in an extensive analysis of the data and of previous studies, concluded that "at best, economic factors can explain about one-fifth of the AFDC caseload changes."[4] Hence, some of the change in numbers of welfare recipients could be attributed to changes in behavior due to the structure of the TANF program.

The TANF program's results have been dramatic, but the program has not entirely eliminated adverse behavioral incentives. Once a household is in poverty, it is eligible for a number of benefits from federal and local governments. Those include such federally subsidized programs as Medicaid, food stamps, school lunch programs, and energy subsidies. Households are also eligible for locally sponsored programs such as day-care centers for children of high school students. Because many of those entitlement programs are open only to low-income households, many women who are heads of households correctly perceive that market employment would entail an enormous income loss, or what is essentially a "tax burden," because of the sacrifice of many of those entitlement benefits.

Although poverty is an important economic indicator where women consistently trail men, it is far from obvious that discrimination in the marketplace is a substantial factor in the incidence of women in poverty or that government programs purporting to reduce sex discrimination in the market would have any noticeable effect on poverty rates. As we discuss below, discrimination in the employment offerings or in the payment of wages to women does not appear to be a central cause of poverty for most women. Indeed, women's poverty appears to be more the confluence of demographic trends and the unintended consequences of government programs.

NOTES

1. See Sally Satel, "There Is No Women's Health Crisis," *The Public Interest*, no. 130 (Winter 1998), pp. 21–33.

2. Data are not available before 1966.

3. For a discussion of the effects of women's careers on childbearing, see Danielle Crittenden, *What Our Mothers Didn't Tell Us: Why Happiness Eludes the Modern Woman* (New York: Simon and Schuster, 1999).

4. Geoffrey Wallace and Rebecca M. Blank, "What Goes Up Must Come Down? Explaining Recent Changes in Public Assistance Caseloads," paper prepared for the Welfare Reform and the Macro Economy conference sponsored by the Joint Center on Poverty Research, October 1998.

PART IV

African American Women

*T*hus far, the statistical analysis presented includes women of all racial backgrounds. African American women deserve special recognition, however, for the enormous legal and social obstacles they have overcome. Their story of economic progress is a testament to the strength of women in the face of adversity.

A Continuing Success Story

The wage gap between men and women, however one may measure it, is far smaller for African Americans than for whites. Figure 4-1 shows a simple measure of an average wage gap, without accounting for education, experience, occupation, position, or full- or part-time work. The average wage gap between African American women and African American men has been consistently smaller than the gap between white women and white men.

Part of the reason for the smaller wage gap for African American women is that over time African American women had higher educational attainment rates than African American men. Figure 4-2 shows that women have accounted for more than half of associate degrees awarded to African Americans over the past twenty years and today account for nearly two-thirds of associate degrees. Figures 4-3 and 4-4 depict an identical pattern for bachelor's and master's degrees, respectively.

In 1977 just over 30 percent of professional degrees among African Americans were awarded to women: by the mid-1990s the women's share had increased to over 55 percent, as figure 4-5 shows. In 1977 women earned almost 40 percent of doctoral degrees

FIGURE 4-1

African American and White Women's Earnings as a Percentage of Men's, 1967–1997

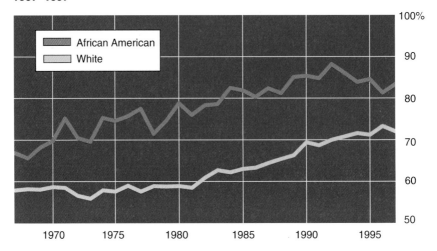

SOURCE: U.S. Census Bureau, *Historical Income Tables,* table P-33, and March *Current Population Survey.*

FIGURE 4-2

Female Percentage of Total Associate's Degrees Awarded to African Americans, 1977–1996

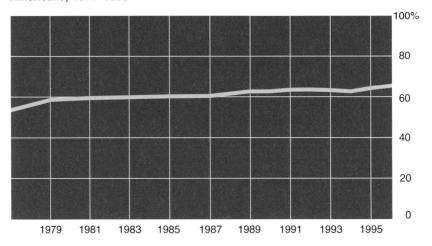

NOTE: Data for 1978, 1980, 1982–1984, 1986, and 1988 are not available.

SOURCE: U.S. Department of Education, National Center for Education Statistics, Integrated Postsecondary Education Data System, "Completions" surveys, 1995–1996, and "Consolidated" survey, 1996; *Digest of Education Statistics,1997,* table 262.

FIGURE 4-3

FIGURE 4-3

Female Percentage of Total Bachelor's Degrees Awarded to African Americans, 1977–1996

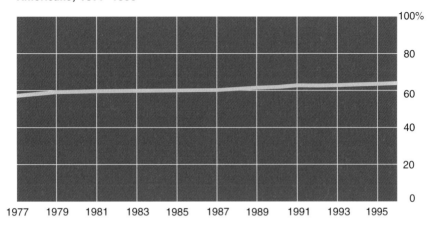

1977   1979   1981   1983   1985   1987   1989   1991   1993   1995

NOTE: Data for 1978, 1980, 1982–1984, 1986, and 1988 are not available.

SOURCE: U.S. Department of Education, National Center for Education Statistics, Integrated Postsecondary Education Data System, "Completions" surveys, 1995–1996, and "Consolidated" survey, 1996; *Digest of Education Statistics, 1997,* table 265.

FIGURE 4-4

Female Percentage of Total Master's Degrees Awarded to African Americans, 1977–1996

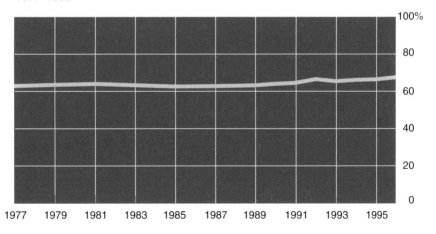

1977   1979   1981   1983   1985   1987   1989   1991   1993   1995

NOTE: Data for 1978, 1980, 1982–1984, 1986, and 1988 are not available.

SOURCE: U.S. Department of Education, National Center for Education Statistics, Integrated Postsecondary Education Data System, "Completions" surveys, 1995–1996, and "Consolidated" survey, 1996; *Digest of Education Statistics, 1997,* table 268.

FIGURE 4-5

Female Percentage of Total First Professional Degrees Awarded to African Americans, 1977–1996

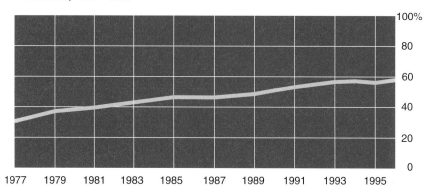

NOTE: Data for 1978, 1980, 1982–1984, 1986, and 1988 are not available.

SOURCE: U.S. Department of Education, National Center for Education Statistics, Integrated Postsecondary Education Data System, "Completions" surveys, 1995–1996, and "Consolidated" survey, 1996; *Digest of Education Statistics, 1997,* table 274.

awarded to African Americans. As figure 4-6 shows, that number increased to 56 percent in 1996.

African American women have also narrowed historically large differences with white women. As recently as 1952, median income for white women was more than two-and-one-half times the median income for African American women. Income differences shrank through the early 1970s, falling below a 10 percent difference in 1972. Median income for African American and white women fluctuated over the past three decades but fell below a 6 percent difference in 1997. Figure 4-7 illustrates those trends.

Earnings differences between African American and white women have been the result of many factors, including education, occupational choice, and racial discrimination. Until the 1950s African American and white women faced separate pay scales. Substantial differences in educational attainment also existed. In 1959 white women in the labor force were twice as likely to have a high school diploma as African American women. By the late 1990s, white women were only 4 percent more likely to have such a qualification, as figure 4-8 shows.

FIGURE 4-6

Female Percentage of Total Doctoral Degrees Awarded to African Americans, 1977–1996

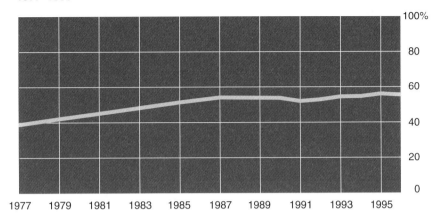

NOTE: Data for 1978, 1980, 1982–1984, 1986, and 1988 are not available.

SOURCE: U.S. Department of Education, National Center for Education Statistics, Integrated Postsecondary Education Data System, "Completions" surveys, 1995–1996, and "Consolidated" survey, 1996; *Digest of Education Statistics, 1997,* table 271.

FIGURE 4-7

Median Income of African American and White Women, 1948–1997

(1997 dollars)

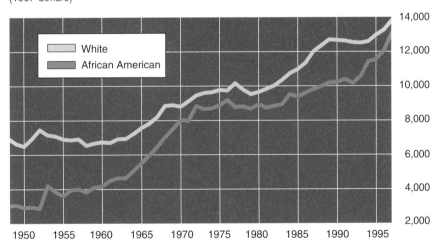

SOURCE: U.S. Census Bureau, *Historical Income Tables*, table P-2, and March *Current Population Survey.*

FIGURE 4-8

Percentage of Female High School Graduates in the Labor Force by Race, 1959–1998

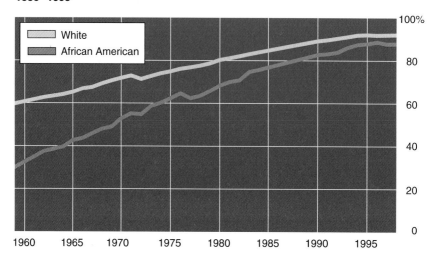

NOTE: Data for 1960, 1961, 1963, and 1985–1989 are not available.

SOURCES: *Handbook of Labor Statistics,* 1985, table 61; Bureau of Labor Statistics, unpublished data from the *Current Population Survey,* annual averages, 1990–1998.

Those and other changes demonstrate that African American women have made enormous strides in the labor market over the past quarter century.

PART
V

Evaluating Claims of Discrimination

*I*t is impossible to untangle the many factors that have contributed to women's economic progress, since they include a strong economic structure that has created many new jobs, complex economic and demographic changes, political and social gains, and expanded personal choices. Legal barriers have fallen, too—a development that enhances women's opportunities for success. This volume challenges the image of women as helpless victims in American society. The statistical evidence shows that American women have achieved startling gains since the early part of the twentieth century: the figures also suggest that they will continue to succeed.

A strong economy is the best antidote for possible discrimination. With an increase in job creation, employers' profits fall if they turn away qualified candidates. The millions of jobs created in the 1980s drew women into the labor force and resulted in many of the advances we observe today. Most of the claims of discrimination against women are made either on grounds of employment discrimination or indirectly through claims of unusually high rates of poverty or other disadvantages for women. While individual instances of sex discrimination may occur, we find little evidence of *systematic* discrimination permeating the economy that would require considerable government intervention to eliminate.

Many remedies are available to combat discrimination. The Equal Pay Act states that women and men working for the same employer in the same establishment and under similar conditions must receive the same pay if their jobs require substantially equal skill, effort, and responsibility. Title VII of the Civil Rights Act of 1964 also prohibits wage discrimination based on sex and provides broader statutory protection of the right to equal pay. The Equal Employment Opportunity Commission is a bipartisan, five-member board charged with eliminating discrimination in employment practices, promoting equal opportunity programs, and investigating complaints of discrimination.

The original intent of many programs to end discrimination and provide equality of opportunity has been transformed into a new objective: equality of results. A set of new government programs, largely labeled under the heading of affirmative action, has debased the intent of the original laws that narrowly addressed equal opportunity. Where individual choices and economic outcomes are not deemed to yield equality of results, affirmative action advocates propose remedies in the form of quotas, preferential treatment, and set-aside programs.

To be sure, supporters of affirmative action programs deny that they seek quotas or preferential treatment. Groups such as the National Association of Women Business Owners claim that their goal is only "equal access." Yet, as our discussion of the "glass ceiling" and the "wage gap" suggests, assessing equal access is a complicated task that must involve a recognition that women often deliberately choose career flexibility or part-time work. The rallying cries of supporters of existing affirmative action programs rarely take such choices into account.

The new affirmative action programs have often looked at career outcomes uncritically. Little conclusive evidence exists that women, with today's equal opportunity, face worse outcomes purely or even partly as the result of sex discrimination. The standard of evidence necessary to demonstrate systematic marketwide sex discrimination against women is rarely if ever met.

Standards of Evidence

The battle for women's rights fought earlier this century focused on blatant discrimination written into statutes and regulations. It culminated in the passage of the Nineteenth Amendment in 1920, granting women the right to vote. Further reforms followed in the form of statutes and regulations that secured equal access for women in education, the professions, and equal status in the eyes of the law. Contemporary battles—supposedly for women's "rights"—are based not on *directly* observable defects of law but on *indirectly* observable differences in outcomes that might result from discrimination against women. According to that perspective, the standard of evidence is equality of outcomes, not equality of opportunities.

While remedies exist for individual acts of sex discrimination, the challenge raised by many women's groups is that unequal outcomes are pervasive and economywide. They claim that failure of our economic system to yield equal outcomes for women and men reflects endemic discrimination. For example, more men become CEOs and more women become nurses, and average wages for women are still lower than those for men. One proposed remedy is further federal government intervention that would provide not just for equal opportunity, but also for equal outcome through such mechanisms as affirmative action and wages set not by economic forces but by federal agencies following "comparable-worth" criteria. Whether such pervasive discrimination exists is an inherently empirical question, but one that cannot be easily answered.

Unfortunately, the claims often rest on indirect rather than direct evidence. It is difficult to determine, for example, whether a woman's failure to reach the position of CEO is due to personal choice, competition from better-qualified candidates, or discrimination. The burden of proof should include the following analytical sequence: first, statistical analysis of market data on the relative performance of men and women in a market; second, the identification of plausible causes for any difference in the performance of men and women; and third, a finding that some or all of the difference in the performance is plausibly the result of harmful discrimination against women.

In practice, however, the contemporary claims for government intervention to help women rarely follow that analytical path. The slightest anecdotal or descriptive evidence is proposed as conclusive of a disparity of market outcomes between men and women. "Women earn only seventy-four cents to the male dollar" is a favorite argument, but it is a statement devoid of context. Which group of women? In what profession? What other factors have been ignored to obtain that figure? Worse still, simple quantitative information, such as wage rates, is sometimes packaged without analysis or interpretation as statistical evidence of a disparity between men and women. The masquerade of basic information as conclusive evidence of the need for government interference for women is what this volume seeks to challenge.

Data cited as evidence of systematic discrimination against women are often imprecise at best and otherwise often misleading and unfounded. The irresponsible use of statistics can lead to harmful results. We live in a world where statistics are a part of our daily lives. They are used to define groups and to determine public policy. When used responsibly, statistics are a valuable map that can guide decisionmakers in their policy determinations. As existing statistics on women demonstrate, however, data can also be used irresponsibly by those who neglect important elements of social topography—personal choices and economic forces, for example—in their assessment of the numbers.

Statistical reasoning does, of course, have an inescapable political dimension. Since the late nineteenth century, when the field of statistics took shape, people have complained bitterly of the biases of numbers. As the cliché suggests, "There are lies, there are damn lies, and there are statistics." Both the phrasing of questions in polling data and the classification of peoples in the census, for example, play an important role in determining the final figures. By far the most important element of statistical reasoning is interpretation. From row upon row of numbers, what questions will be asked? How nuanced an analysis will the translator perform?

Furthermore, even if one could find plausibly harmful discrimination against women in the data, government interference is not always the logical or successful remedy. Most statutory and regulatory discrimination against women has already been addressed in the legal realm; the easy changes have been made. Statutory changes are at best a blunt instrument to remedy alleged discrimination that results from unobservable social conditions. The results of the blunt instrument may well be imprecise, inefficient, and ineffective.

PART
VI

Conclusion

Since the earliest years of the twentieth century, American women have sought equal opportunities in education, the labor force, and the eyes of the law. In this volume we have shown that in most of those areas women have achieved that equality. They are well represented in the professions, and they continue to enter fields of study that were previously dominated by men. Women are starting their own businesses and winning elective offices throughout the country. Laws barring discrimination against women are on the books and enforced. All those gains clearly belie the image of women as victims struggling against discrimination in the workplace.

We have challenged the image of women as victims because it contradicts the obvious statistical gains American women have made in the twentieth century. It is also not an image with which most women identify. The countless women who have won elective office and made it to the top of their professions are not victims. They are evidence of just how far American women have come and how far they are going.

Many factors have contributed to that record of achievement. The reform efforts of suffragists in the nineteenth and early twentieth centuries were important, as were those of the feminists of the 1960s. American women owe a great deal to those who fought for the passage of civil rights legislation in the 1960s, particularly the Equal Pay Act of 1963 and the Civil Rights Act of 1964. Demographic and economic trends also shaped women's experiences.

The personal choices women have made are perhaps the most important and least appreciated factor in women's economic progress over the years. Decisions to enter previously male-dominated fields of education and employment, to marry and bear children later in life, to join the work force, and to leave the work force to raise children have all had an enormous effect on whether women can achieve total parity with men. Some of those choices, such as leaving the work force for a time to raise children or working part-time, have a negative effect on women's earnings. Others, such as entering previously all-male fields, have led to remarkable gains for women in the work force.

Unfortunately, that ambiguous legacy of choice is often ignored in favor of an image of women as victims of widespread discrimination. Such a portrayal of women overlooks an important factor: the possibility that many women do not want to reach the top of the corporate ladder. The mass media uncritically accept as the standard of equality the requirement that women's achievements be statistically identical to men's achievements in all areas. That standard is insidious: it suggests that something is wrong if women do not earn the highest salaries. That is insulting to all workers who choose flexibility, a friendly workplace environment, and other nonmonetary factors in the course of their careers.

Challenging those long-held assumptions about women is a perilous exercise, particularly because many groups have an investment in maintaining myths such as the wage gap and the glass ceiling. Both the wage gap and the glass ceiling are rhetorically useful but factually corrupt catch phrases. As we have demonstrated, those myths are harmful to women and do little to describe accurately the complex factors that determine a woman's place in the labor market. Important elements such as experience, intensity of work effort, and field of employment are not taken into consideration by those who generate pessimistic statistics about women's lack of progress. In addition, those who constantly point to the existence of a wage gap and a glass ceiling ignore one of the most important (but least statistically measurable) factors: personal choice.

The heterogeneity of the female population in this country guarantees that women will never reach consensus on all issues. From a statistical perspective, however, women have clearly made impressive gains: levels of education, wages, entrepreneurship, and employment have increased dramatically in the past several decades, and they will continue to improve. We have argued throughout this volume that although women faced discrimination in the past, that is only a small part of the story. The rest is a success story, and one that deserves to be told.

APPENDIX

Statistical Tables

*T*his appendix presents tables that provide the data points for the figures in Parts Two, Three, and Four. The table numbers correspond to the figure numbers.

TABLE A2-1

Estimated Average Usual Weekly Earnings of Women as a Percentage of Men's Earnings, 1974–1993

Year	Ages 16–29	Ages 30–40	Ages 45+	Year	Ages 16–29	Ages 30–40	Ages 45+
1974	77	62	60	1985	83	67	60
1976	78	61	61	1986	83	68	60
1978	77	61	59	1987	84	70	59
1979	77	63	60	1988	85	70	61
1980	78	63	60	1989	86	73	63
1981	79	65	59	1990	88	74	64
1982	80	65	60	1991	89	75	66
1983	82	66	58	1992	90	78	67
1984	81	67	59	1993	92	78	67

NOTE: Data for 1975 and 1977 are not available.

SOURCE: David A. Macpherson and Barry T. Hirsch, "Wages and Gender Composition: Why Do Women's Jobs Pay Less?" *Journal of Labor Economics*, vol. 13 (July 1995), p. 466, table A1.

TABLE A2-2

Female-Male Wage Ratios at Age 30, 1980 and 1991

Year	Mothers	Childless Women
1980	.60	.72
1991	.75	.95

SOURCE: Jane Waldfogel, "Working Mothers Then and Now: Effects of Maternity Leave on Women's Pay," in Francine Blau and Ronald Ehrenberg, eds., *Gender and Family Issues in the Workplace* (New York: Russell Sage Foundation, 1997).

TABLE A2-3

Women as a Percentage of Total Employment by Occupation, 1983 and 1997

Occupation	1983	1997
Public administration official	36.2	49.5
Financial manager	38.0	49.3
Accountant or auditor	40.7	56.6
Insurance underwriter	42.6	70.1
Health or medicine manager	60.7	76.8

Source: U.S. Department of Labor, Bureau of Labor Statistics, unpublished tabulation from the *Current Population Survey.*

TABLE A2-4

Unemployment Rates by Sex, 1940–1997

Year	Men	Women	Year	Men	Women	Year	Men	Women
1940	13.0	15.5	1960	5.4	5.9	1980	6.9	7.4
1941	9.5	11.2	1961	6.4	7.2	1981	7.4	7.9
1942	4.3	5.8	1962	5.2	6.2	1982	9.9	9.4
1943	1.5	2.7	1963	5.2	6.5	1983	9.9	9.2
1944	1.0	1.7	1964	4.6	6.2	1984	7.4	7.6
1945	1.8	2.2	1965	4.0	5.5	1985	7.0	7.4
1946	4.4	2.8	1966	3.2	4.8	1986	6.9	7.1
1947	4.0	3.7	1967	3.1	5.2	1987	6.2	6.2
1948	3.6	4.1	1968	2.9	4.8	1988	5.5	5.6
1949	5.9	6.0	1969	2.8	4.7	1989	5.2	5.4
1950	5.1	5.7	1970	4.4	5.9	1990	5.6	5.4
1951	2.8	4.4	1971	5.3	6.9	1991	7.0	6.3
1952	2.8	3.6	1972	4.9	6.6	1992	7.8	6.9
1953	2.8	3.3	1973	4.1	6.0	1993	7.1	6.5
1954	5.3	6.0	1974	4.8	6.7	1994	6.2	6.0
1955	4.2	4.9	1975	7.9	9.3	1995	5.6	5.6
1956	3.8	4.8	1976	7.0	8.6	1996	5.4	5.4
1957	4.1	4.7	1977	6.2	8.2	1997	4.9	5.0
1958	6.8	6.8	1978	5.2	7.2			
1959	5.3	5.9	1979	5.1	6.8			

NOTES: Data beginning for 1994 are not directly comparable with earlier years. Data for 1940–1946 include ages fourteen and older; starting in 1947, data include ages sixteen and older. Beginning in January 1997, data reflect revised population controls used in the household.

SOURCES: *Historical Statistics,* vol. 1, D11-25, pp. 127–28. *Statistical Abstract:* 1950, no. 209; 1977, no. 627; 1979, no. 647; 1988, no. 647; 1991, no. 635; 1994, no. 616; 1995, no. 628. *Employment and Earnings:* January 1997, p. 193, table 24; January 1998, p. 196, table 24.

TABLE A2-5

Percentage of Associate's Degrees Awarded to Women, 1966–1996

Year	%	Year	%	Year	%	Year	%
1966	42.9	1974	45.2	1982	54.7	1990	58.0
1967	43.7	1975	47.0	1983	54.6	1991	60.0
1968	43.6	1976	46.4	1984	55.2	1992	58.9
1969	42.3	1977	48.1	1985	55.4	1993	58.8
1970	43.0	1978	50.3	1986	56.0	1994	59.3
1971	42.9	1979	52.3	1987	56.3	1995	59.5
1972	43.1	1980	54.2	1988	56.3	1996	60.5
1973	44.5	1981	54.7	1989	57.3		

SOURCE: U.S. Department of Education, National Center for Education Statistics, Integrated Postsecondary Education Data System, "Completions" surveys.

TABLE A2-6

Percentage of Bachelor's Degrees Awarded to Women, 1920–1996

Year	%	Year	%	Year	%	Year	%
1920	34.2	1950	23.9	1966	42.5	1982	50.3
1922	33.0	1951	27.3	1967	42.2	1983	50.6
1924	33.7	1952	31.5	1968	43.4	1984	50.5
1926	36.0	1953	34.1	1969	43.7	1985	50.7
1928	39.1	1954	35.9	1970	43.1	1986	50.8
1930	39.9	1955	36.0	1971	43.4	1987	51.5
1932	39.7	1956	35.8	1972	43.8	1988	52.0
1934	39.5	1957	34.5	1973	43.8	1989	52.6
1936	39.9	1958	33.5	1974	44.2	1990	53.2
1938	40.8	1959	33.5	1975	45.3	1991	53.9
1940	40.8	1960	35.3	1976	45.5	1992	54.2
1942	43.9	1961	38.5	1977	46.1	1993	54.3
1944	55.6	1962	40.0	1978	47.1	1994	54.5
1946	56.9	1963	41.3	1979	48.2	1995	54.6
1948	35.2	1964	42.5	1980	49.0	1996	55.1
1949	27.9	1965	42.9	1981	49.8		

Note: Data for odd years from 1921 to 1947 are not available.

Source: U.S. Department of Education, National Center for Education Statistics, Integrated Postsecondary Education Data System, "Completions" surveys.

TABLE A2-7

Percentage of Master's Degrees Awarded to Women, 1920–1996

Year	%	Year	%	Year	%	Year	%
1920	30.2	1950	29.2	1966	33.8	1982	50.7
1922	28.1	1951	29.0	1967	34.6	1983	50.1
1924	32.9	1952	31.4	1968	35.8	1984	49.5
1926	36.3	1953	32.8	1969	37.3	1985	49.9
1928	37.6	1954	31.7	1970	39.7	1986	50.3
1930	40.4	1955	33.4	1971	40.1	1987	51.2
1932	37.0	1956	33.5	1972	40.6	1988	51.5
1934	37.0	1957	33.5	1973	41.3	1989	51.9
1936	37.1	1958	32.6	1974	43.0	1990	52.6
1938	38.0	1959	33.3	1975	44.8	1991	53.6
1940	38.2	1960	31.6	1976	46.4	1992	54.3
1942	42.5	1961	31.7	1977	47.1	1993	54.2
1944	57.4	1962	31.5	1978	48.3	1994	54.5
1946	50.6	1963	31.8	1979	49.1	1995	55.1
1948	31.8	1964	32.4	1980	49.4	1996	55.9
1949	30.6	1965	32.9	1981	50.3		

NOTE: Data for odd years from 1921 to 1947 are not available.

SOURCE: U.S. Department of Education, National Center for Education Statistics, Integrated Postsecondary Education Data System, "Completions" surveys.

TABLE A2-8

Percentage of Doctoral Degrees Awarded to Women, 1920–1996

Year	%	Year	%	Year	%	Year	%
1920	15.1	1950	9.6	1966	11.6	1982	32.1
1922	15.3	1951	9.2	1967	11.9	1983	33.2
1924	14.5	1952	9.3	1968	12.6	1984	33.6
1926	13.7	1953	9.5	1969	12.2	1985	34.1
1928	13.7	1954	9.1	1970	13.3	1986	34.9
1930	15.4	1955	9.3	1971	14.3	1987	35.2
1932	15.3	1956	9.9	1972	15.8	1988	35.1
1934	13.2	1957	10.7	1973	17.9	1989	36.6
1936	14.4	1958	10.8	1974	19.1	1990	36.1
1938	14.7	1959	10.4	1975	21.3	1991	38.0
1940	13.0	1960	10.5	1976	22.9	1992	37.2
1942	13.2	1961	10.5	1977	24.3	1993	37.2
1944	18.4	1962	10.7	1978	26.4	1994	38.5
1946	19.6	1963	10.7	1979	28.1	1995	39.4
1948	12.4	1964	10.6	1980	29.7	1996	39.9
1949	10.3	1965	10.8	1981	31.1		

NOTE: Data for odd years from 1921 to 1947 are not available.

SOURCE: U.S. Department of Education, National Center for Education Statistics, Integrated Postsecondary Education Data System, "Completions" surveys.

TABLE A2-9

Percentage of First Professional Degrees Awarded to Women, 1961–1996

Year	%	Year	%	Year	%	Year	%
1961	2.7	1970	5.3	1979	23.5	1988	35.7
1962	3.0	1971	6.3	1980	24.8	1989	36.4
1963	3.1	1972	6.2	1981	26.6	1990	38.1
1964	3.1	1973	7.1	1982	27.5	1991	39.1
1965	3.6	1974	9.8	1983	29.8	1992	39.2
1966	3.8	1975	12.4	1984	31.0	1993	40.1
1967	4.1	1976	15.6	1985	32.8	1994	40.7
1968	4.5	1977	18.6	1986	33.2	1995	40.8
1969	4.3	1978	21.5	1987	35.0	1996	41.7

NOTE: First professional degrees are defined as requiring at least two years of college and a total of six years of schooling and certify an individual to practice a particular profession. First professional degrees are conferred in the fields of chiropractic medicine, dentistry, law, medicine, osteopathic medicine, pharmacy, podiatry, theology, and veterinary medicine.

SOURCE: U.S. Department of Education, National Center for Education Statistics, Integrated Postsecondary Education Data System, "Completions" surveys.

TABLE A2-10

Percentage of Master's Degrees in Business Awarded to Women, 1956–1996

Year	%	Year	%	Year	%	Year	%
1956	4.9	1972	3.9	1981	25.1	1990	34.0
1958	3.6	1973	4.9	1982	27.9	1991	35.0
1960	3.6	1974	6.6	1983	29.0	1992	35.4
1962	2.7	1975	8.5	1984	30.2	1993	35.7
1964	2.6	1976	11.7	1985	31.0	1994	36.5
1966	2.6	1977	14.4	1986	31.1	1995	37.0
1968	3.4	1978	16.9	1987	33.1	1996	37.5
1970	3.6	1979	19.2	1988	33.6		
1971	3.9	1980	22.4	1989	33.6		

NOTE: Includes degrees in business management/administrative services, marketing operations/ marketing and distribution, and consumer and personal services. Data for odd years from 1957 to 1969 are not available.

SOURCE: U.S. Department of Education, National Center for Education Statistics, Higher Education General Information Survey, "Degrees and Other Formal Awards Conferred" surveys, and Integrated Postsecondary Education Data System, "Completions" surveys.

TABLE A2-11

Percentage of Law Degrees Awarded to Women, 1956–1996

Year	%	Year	%	Year	%	Year	%
1956	3.5	1972	6.9	1981	32.4	1990	42.2
1958	2.9	1973	8.0	1982	33.4	1991	43.0
1960	2.5	1974	11.4	1983	36.1	1992	42.7
1962	2.9	1975	15.1	1984	36.8	1993	42.5
1964	2.9	1976	19.2	1985	38.0	1994	43.0
1966	3.5	1977	22.5	1986	38.5	1995	42.6
1968	3.9	1978	26.0	1987	40.2	1996	43.5
1970	5.4	1979	28.5	1988	40.5		
1971	7.1	1980	30.2	1989	40.9		

NOTE: Data for odd years from 1957 to 1969 are not available.

SOURCE: U.S. Department of Education, National Center for Education Statistics, "Degrees and Other Formal Awards Conferred" surveys, and Integrated Postsecondary Education Data System, "Completions" surveys.

TABLE A2-12

Percentage of Dentistry Degrees Awarded to Women, 1950–1996

Year	%	Year	%	Year	%	Year	%
1950	0.7	1970	0.9	1980	13.3	1990	30.9
1952	0.8	1971	1.1	1981	14.4	1991	32.1
1954	1.3	1972	1.1	1982	15.4	1992	32.3
1956	1.1	1973	1.4	1983	17.1	1993	33.9
1958	1.1	1974	1.9	1984	19.6	1994	38.5
1960	0.8	1975	3.1	1985	20.7	1995	36.4
1962	0.5	1976	4.4	1986	21.9	1996	35.8
1964	0.4	1977	7.3	1987	24.0		
1966	1.0	1978	10.9	1988	26.3		
1968	1.4	1979	11.8	1989	26.8		

NOTE: Data for odd years from 1951 to 1969 are not available.

SOURCE: U.S. Department of Education, National Center for Education Statistics, "Degrees and Other Formal Awards Conferred" surveys, and Integrated Postsecondary Education Data System, "Completions" surveys.

TABLE A2-13

Percentage of Medical Degrees Awarded to Women, 1950–1996

Year	%	Year	%	Year	%	Year	%
1950	10.4	1970	8.4	1980	23.4	1990	34.2
1952	5.3	1971	9.1	1981	24.7	1991	36.0
1954	5.0	1972	9.0	1982	25.0	1992	35.3
1956	5.1	1973	8.9	1983	26.7	1993	37.7
1958	5.1	1974	11.3	1984	28.2	1994	37.9
1960	5.5	1975	13.1	1985	30.4	1995	38.8
1962	5.5	1976	16.2	1986	30.4	1996	40.9
1964	5.8	1977	19.1	1987	32.4		
1966	6.6	1978	21.5	1988	33.1		
1968	7.9	1979	23.0	1989	33.3		

NOTE: Data for odd years from 1951 to 1969 are not available.

SOURCE: U.S. Department of Education, National Center for Education Statistics, "Degrees and Other Formal Awards Conferred" surveys, and Integrated Postsecondary Education Data System, "Completions" surveys.

TABLE A2-14

Percentage of Adult Women Who Work, 1940–1997

Year	%	Year	%	Year	%	Year	%
1940	25.8	1955	35.7	1970	43.3	1985	54.5
1941	28.5	1956	36.9	1971	43.4	1986	55.3
1942	30.9	1957	36.9	1972	43.9	1987	56.0
1943	35.7	1958	37.1	1973	44.7	1988	56.6
1944	36.3	1959	37.1	1974	45.7	1989	57.4
1945	35.8	1960	37.7	1975	46.3	1990	57.5
1946	30.8	1961	38.1	1976	47.3	1991	57.3
1947	31.8	1962	37.9	1977	48.4	1992	57.8
1948	32.7	1963	38.3	1978	50.0	1993	57.9
1949	33.1	1964	38.7	1979	50.9	1994	58.8
1950	33.9	1965	39.3	1980	51.5	1995	58.9
1951	34.6	1966	40.3	1981	52.1	1996	59.3
1952	34.7	1967	41.1	1982	52.6	1997	59.8
1953	34.4	1968	41.6	1983	52.9		
1954	34.6	1969	42.7	1984	53.6		

SOURCES: *Handbook of Labor Statistics,* 1988, table 5; *Historical Statistics,* vol. 1, series A, pp. 119–34, series D, pp. 29–41; *Statistical Abstract:* 1988, no. 625; 1993, no. 622; 1994, no. 615; and *Employment and Earnings,* vols. 43–45, no. 1, annual averages, table 3.

TABLE A2-15

Distribution of Female Labor Force by Educational Attainment, 1952–1998

Year	< High School	High School Graduate	1–3 Years College	4+ Years College
1952	49.0	33.8	8.8	7.7
1957	45.4	36.1	9.1	8.2
1959	44.1	38.1	9.7	8.1
1962	40.6	38.7	11.2	9.5
1964	39.0	40.9	10.6	9.5
1965	37.7	41.9	10.4	10.0
1966	36.2	43.0	11.0	9.9
1967	35.4	42.9	11.8	9.9
1968	33.6	43.7	12.3	10.5
1969	32.2	45.0	12.4	10.4
1970	33.5	44.3	10.9	11.2
1971	32.2	44.2	11.9	11.8
1972	30.7	45.1	11.8	12.4
1973	28.4	45.9	12.4	13.3
1974	26.7	45.3	13.4	14.6
1975	26.5	45.5	13.9	14.1
1976	24.0	45.1	14.7	16.2
1977	22.8	45.1	15.2	16.9
1978	22.0	44.9	16.1	17.0
1979	20.1	45.0	17.1	17.8
1980	18.4	45.4	17.4	18.7
1981	17.4	46.1	17.9	18.6
1982	16.6	45.6	18.3	19.5
1983	15.6	44.8	18.8	20.9
1984	14.5	44.9	18.9	21.7
1985	13.7	44.4	19.9	22.0
1986	13.2	44.3	20.3	22.2
1987	12.5	44.0	20.7	22.8
1988	12.4	43.3	21.2	23.1
1989	11.9	42.9	20.9	24.3
1990	11.2	42.1	22.1	24.6
1991	10.7	41.8	22.5	25.0
1992	10.6	37.6	27.1	24.8
1993	9.6	36.7	28.2	25.5
1994	9.0	35.0	29.8	26.2
1995	8.8	34.1	30.2	26.9
1996	8.8	33.6	29.9	27.8
1997	8.7	33.5	29.4	28.4
1998	8.8	32.7	29.4	29.2

NOTE: Data for 1953–1956, 1958, 1960–1961, and 1963 are not available.

SOURCES: *Statistical Abstract:* 1991, no. 634; 1994, no. 617; *Handbook of Labor Statistics:* 1967, table 8; 1985, table 61; 1989, table 65; Bureau of Labor Statistics, unpublished data from the *Current Population Survey,* annual averages, 1992, 1993, 1994, 1995, 1996, 1997, and 1998.

TABLE A2-16

Percentage of Labor Force That Is Women, 1948–1998

Year	%	Year	%	Year	%	Year	%
1948	28.5	1961	33.6	1974	38.9	1987	44.8
1949	29.0	1962	33.8	1975	39.6	1988	45.0
1950	29.4	1963	34.1	1976	40.1	1989	45.2
1951	30.3	1964	34.4	1977	40.5	1990	45.2
1952	30.8	1965	34.8	1978	41.2	1991	45.4
1953	30.7	1966	35.6	1979	41.7	1992	45.6
1954	30.7	1967	36.2	1980	42.4	1993	45.7
1955	31.4	1968	36.6	1981	42.8	1994	46.0
1956	32.0	1969	37.3	1982	43.5	1995	46.1
1957	32.3	1970	37.7	1983	43.7	1996	46.2
1958	32.7	1971	37.8	1984	43.7	1997	46.2
1959	32.7	1972	38.1	1985	44.1	1998	46.2
1960	33.3	1973	38.5	1986	44.4		

NOTE: Data for 1994–1996 are not strictly comparable with prior years owing to the introduction of a redesigned *Current Population Survey* questionnaire. Beginning in 1997, data are not strictly comparable with prior years because of revisions in the population controls used in the household survey.

SOURCE: U.S. Department of Labor, Bureau of Labor Statistics.

TABLE A2-17

Total Employment by Sex, 1948–1998 (millions of workers)

Year	Women	Men	Year	Women	Men	Year	Women	Men
1948	16.6	41.7	1965	24.7	46.3	1982	43.3	56.3
1949	16.8	40.9	1966	26.0	46.9	1983	44.0	56.8
1950	17.3	41.6	1967	26.9	47.5	1984	45.9	59.1
1951	18.2	41.8	1968	27.8	48.1	1985	47.3	59.9
1952	18.6	41.7	1969	29.1	48.8	1986	48.7	60.9
1953	18.8	42.4	1970	29.7	49.0	1987	50.3	62.1
1954	18.5	41.6	1971	30.0	49.4	1988	51.7	63.3
1955	19.5	42.6	1972	31.3	50.9	1989	53.0	64.3
1956	20.4	43.4	1973	32.7	52.3	1990	53.7	65.1
1957	20.7	43.3	1974	33.8	53.0	1991	53.5	64.2
1958	20.6	42.4	1975	34.0	51.8	1992	54.1	64.4
1959	21.2	43.5	1976	35.6	53.1	1993	54.9	65.4
1960	21.9	43.9	1977	37.3	54.7	1994	56.6	66.5
1961	22.1	43.7	1978	39.6	56.5	1995	57.5	67.4
1962	22.5	44.2	1979	41.2	57.6	1996	58.5	68.2
1963	23.1	44.7	1980	42.1	57.2	1997	59.9	69.7
1964	23.8	45.5	1981	43.0	57.4	1998	60.8	70.7

NOTE: Data for 1994–1996 are not strictly comparable with prior years owing to the introduction of a redesigned *Current Population Survey* questionnaire. Beginning in 1997, data are not strictly comparable with prior years because of revisions in the population controls used in the household survey.

SOURCE: U.S. Department of Labor, Bureau of Labor Statistics.

TABLE A2-18

Full-Time Employment by Sex, 1968–1997

(millions of workers)

Year	Men	Women	Year	Men	Women	Year	Men	Women
1968	44.4	20.9	1978	51.3	28.9	1988	56.8	38.4
1969	44.8	21.8	1979	52.4	30.2	1989	57.9	39.5
1970	44.8	21.9	1980	51.7	30.8	1990	58.0	40.0
1971	45.0	22.0	1981	51.9	31.3	1991	56.9	39.6
1972	46.4	22.8	1982	50.3	31.1	1992	56.9	40.1
1973	47.8	24.0	1983	50.6	31.7	1993	57.6	40.8
1974	48.4	24.7	1984	53.1	33.5	1994	58.8	40.9
1975	47.0	24.6	1985	53.9	34.7	1995	59.9	41.7
1976	48.2	25.8	1986	54.7	35.8	1996	60.7	43.3
1977	49.6	27.1	1987	55.7	37.2	1997	62.1	44.5

NOTE: Data for 1994–1996 are not strictly comparable with prior years owing to the introduction of a redesigned *Current Population Survey* questionnaire. Beginning in 1997, data reflect revised population controls used in the household survey.

SOURCES: U.S. Bureau of the Census, *Current Population Survey;* U.S. Department of Labor, Bureau of Labor Statistics, *Employment and Earnings.*

TABLE A2-19

Part-Time Employment by Sex, 1968–1997

(millions of workers)

Year	Men	Women	Year	Men	Women	Year	Men	Women
1968	3.7	6.9	1978	5.2	10.7	1988	6.5	13.3
1969	4.0	7.3	1979	5.2	11.0	1989	6.4	13.5
1970	4.2	7.8	1980	5.5	11.3	1990	6.5	13.5
1971	4.4	8.0	1981	5.5	11.7	1991	6.7	13.6
1972	4.5	8.4	1982	5.9	12.2	1992	6.9	13.7
1973	4.5	8.8	1983	6.1	12.4	1993	7.1	13.8
1974	4.6	9.1	1984	6.0	12.4	1994	7.6	15.7
1975	4.9	9.4	1985	6.0	12.6	1995	7.4	15.8
1976	5.0	9.8	1986	6.2	12.9	1996	7.7	16.2
1977	5.2	10.2	1987	6.4	13.1	1997	7.7	16.4

NOTE: Data for 1994–1996 are not strictly comparable with prior years owing to the introduction of a redesigned *Current Population Survey* questionnaire. Beginning in 1997, data reflect revised population controls used in the household survey.

SOURCES: U.S. Bureau of the Census, *Current Population Survey;* U.S. Department of Labor, Bureau of Labor Statistics, *Employment and Earnings.*

TABLE A2-20

Percentage of Women in the Labor Force by Marital Status, 1947–1997

Year	Single (never married)	Married (spouse present)	Year	Single (never married)	Married (spouse present)
1947	51.2	20.0	1973	55.9	42.2
1948	51.1	22.0	1974	57.4	43.1
1949	50.9	22.5	1975	57.0	44.4
1950	50.5	23.8	1976	59.2	45.1
1951	49.8	25.2	1977	59.2	46.6
1952	50.0	25.3	1978	60.7	47.5
1953	48.5	26.3	1979	62.9	49.3
1954	49.0	26.6	1980	61.5	50.1
1955	46.4	27.7	1981	62.3	51.0
1956	46.4	29.0	1982	62.2	51.2
1957	46.8	29.6	1983	62.6	51.8
1958	45.4	30.2	1984	63.1	52.8
1959	43.4	30.9	1985	65.2	54.2
1960	44.1	30.5	1986	65.3	54.6
1961	44.4	32.7	1987	65.1	55.8
1962	41.7	32.7	1988	65.2	56.5
1963	41.0	33.7	1989	66.4	58.2
1964	40.9	34.4	1990	66.1	58.5
1965	40.5	34.7	1991	64.7	59.3
1966	40.8	35.4	1992	64.5	59.4
1967	50.7	36.8	1993	65.1	60.6
1968	51.3	38.3	1994	65.5	61.1
1969	51.2	39.6	1995	65.5	61.1
1970	53.0	40.8	1996	65.2	61.1
1971	52.8	40.8	1997	66.8	62.1
1972	55.0	41.5			

NOTES: Data for 1947–1966 include women fourteen years old and older. Beginning in 1967, all data refer to women ages sixteen and older. Single teenagers not in the labor force may be in school.

SOURCES: U.S. Department of Labor, Bureau of Labor Statistics, unpublished tabulations from the *Current Population Survey; Statistical Abstract*, 1995, no. 637.

Number of Women-Owned Businesses, 1972–1997
(millions)

Year	All Industries, All Firms	Year	All Industries, All Firms
1972	0.40	1987	4.11
1977	0.70	1992	6.41
1982	2.61	1997	8.47

NOTE: Data for 1992 and 1997 include C corporations.

SOURCES: U.S. Bureau of the Census, *Economic Census*, "Women-Owned Businesses," 1977, table 1; 1987, table 1. U.S. Small Business Administration, Office of Advocacy, *Women in Business*, October 1998, table 1, 1992 and 1997.

TABLE A2-22
Industry Distribution of Women-Owned Firms, 1996

Industry	%	Industry	%
Services	52	Goods producing	9
Retail	19	Other	10
Finance, insurance, real estate	10		

NOTE: Goods-producing industries are defined as agriculture, manufacturing, and construction.

SOURCE: National Foundation for Women Business Owners, "Facts on Women-Owned Businesses, State Trends," 1996.

TABLE A2-23
Number of Women Candidates for U.S. Congressional Offices, 1968–1998

Year	Total	Year	Total	Year	Total	Year	Total
1968	20	1976	55	1984	75	1992	117
1970	26	1978	48	1986	70	1994	121
1972	34	1980	57	1988	61	1996	129
1974	47	1982	58	1990	77	1998	131

NOTES: Data include minor party candidates only if their parties have recently won statewide offices. Data after 1990 do not include the delegates from Washington, D.C., and the five territories.

SOURCE: Center for the American Woman and Politics, Eagleton Institute of Politics, Rutgers University.

TABLE A2-24

Number of Women in the U.S. Congress, 1917–1999

Year	Total	Year	Total	Year	Total	Year	Total
1917	1	1939	9	1961	20	1983	24
1919	0	1941	10	1963	14	1985	25
1921	4	1943	9	1965	13	1987	25
1923	1	1945	11	1967	12	1989	31
1925	3	1947	8	1969	11	1991	32
1927	5	1949	10	1971	15	1993	54
1929	9	1951	11	1973	16	1995	55
1931	8	1953	13	1975	19	1997	63
1933	8	1955	17	1977	20	1999	65
1935	8	1957	16	1979	17		
1937	8	1959	19	1981	23		

NOTES: Table shows maximum number of women elected or appointed to serve in that Congress at one time period. Some filled out unexpired terms, and some were never sworn in.

SOURCE: Center for the American Woman and Politics, Eagleton Institute of Politics, Rutgers University.

TABLE A3-1

Life Expectancy at Birth by Sex, 1920–1996

(age in years)

Year	Men	Women	Year	Men	Women	Year	Men	Women
1920	53.6	54.6	1946	64.4	69.4	1972	67.4	75.1
1921	60.0	61.8	1947	64.4	69.7	1973	67.6	75.3
1922	58.4	61.0	1948	64.6	69.9	1974	68.2	75.9
1923	56.1	58.5	1949	65.2	70.7	1975	68.8	76.6
1924	58.1	61.5	1950	65.6	71.7	1976	69.1	76.8
1925	57.6	60.6	1951	65.6	71.4	1977	69.5	77.2
1926	55.5	58.0	1952	65.8	71.6	1978	69.6	77.3
1927	59.0	62.1	1953	66.0	72.0	1979	70.0	77.8
1928	55.6	58.3	1954	66.7	72.8	1980	70.0	77.4
1929	55.8	58.7	1955	66.7	72.8	1981	70.4	77.8
1930	58.1	61.6	1956	66.7	72.9	1982	70.9	78.1
1931	59.4	63.1	1957	66.4	72.7	1983	71.0	78.1
1932	61.0	63.5	1958	66.6	72.9	1984	71.1	78.2
1933	61.7	65.1	1959	66.8	73.2	1985	71.1	78.2
1934	59.3	63.3	1960	66.6	73.1	1986	71.2	78.2
1935	59.9	63.9	1961	67.0	73.6	1987	71.4	78.3
1936	56.6	60.6	1962	66.8	73.4	1988	71.4	78.3
1937	58.0	62.4	1963	66.6	73.4	1989	71.7	78.5
1938	61.9	65.3	1964	66.9	73.7	1990	71.8	78.8
1939	62.1	65.4	1965	66.8	73.7	1991	72.0	78.9
1940	60.8	65.2	1966	66.7	73.8	1992	72.3	79.1
1941	63.1	66.8	1967	67.0	74.2	1993	72.2	78.8
1942	64.7	67.9	1968	66.6	74.0	1994	72.3	79.0
1943	62.4	64.4	1969	66.8	74.3	1995	72.5	78.9
1944	63.6	66.8	1970	67.1	74.8	1996	73.0	79.0
1945	63.6	67.9	1971	67.4	75.0			

SOURCES: *Historical Statistics,* vol. 1, series B, pp.107–15; *Statistical Abstract,* 1998, no. 128; *Vital Statistics,* 1985, no. 102; *World Almanac,* 1998, p. 973.

TABLE A3-2

Percentage of Population below Poverty Line by Sex, 1966–1997

Year	Men	Women	Year	Men	Women	Year	Men	Women
1966	13	16	1977	10	13	1988	12	14
1967	13	16	1978	10	13	1989	11	14
1968	11	14	1979	10	13	1990	12	15
1969	11	14	1980	11	15	1991	12	16
1970	11	14	1981	12	16	1992	13	17
1971	11	14	1982	13	17	1993	13	17
1972	10	13	1983	14	17	1994	13	16
1973	10	13	1984	13	16	1995	12	15
1974	10	13	1985	12	16	1996	12	15
1975	11	14	1986	12	15	1997	12	15
1976	10	13	1987	12	15			

SOURCE: U.S. Bureau of the Census, *Current Population Survey.*

TABLE A3-3

Median Age at First Marriage by Sex, 1947–1998

(age in years)

Year	Men	Women	Year	Men	Women	Year	Men	Women
1947	23.7	20.5	1965	22.8	20.6	1983	25.4	22.8
1948	23.3	20.4	1966	22.8	20.5	1984	25.4	23.0
1949	22.7	20.3	1967	23.1	20.6	1985	25.5	23.3
1950	22.8	20.3	1968	23.1	20.8	1986	25.7	23.1
1951	22.9	20.4	1969	23.2	20.8	1987	25.8	23.6
1952	23.0	20.2	1970	23.2	20.8	1988	25.9	23.6
1953	22.8	20.2	1971	23.1	20.9	1989	26.2	23.8
1954	23.0	20.3	1972	23.3	20.9	1990	26.1	23.9
1955	22.6	20.2	1973	23.2	21.0	1991	26.3	24.1
1956	22.5	20.1	1974	23.1	21.1	1992	26.5	24.4
1957	22.6	20.3	1975	23.5	21.1	1993	26.5	24.5
1958	22.6	20.2	1976	23.8	21.3	1994	26.7	24.5
1959	22.5	20.2	1977	24.0	21.6	1995	26.9	24.5
1960	22.8	20.3	1978	24.2	21.8	1996	27.1	24.8
1961	22.8	20.3	1979	24.4	22.1	1997	26.8	25.0
1962	22.7	20.3	1980	24.7	22.0	1998	26.7	25.0
1963	22.8	20.5	1981	24.8	22.3			
1964	23.1	20.5	1982	25.2	22.5			

SOURCE: U.S. Bureau of the Census, *Current Population Reports,* series P20-514, "Marital Status and Living Arrangements: March 1998 (Update)," and earlier reports.

TABLE A3-4

Divorce Rates per 1,000 Married Women, 1920–1997

Year	Rate	Year	Rate	Year	Rate	Year	Rate
1920	8.0	1940	8.8	1960	9.2	1980	22.6
1921	7.2	1941	9.4	1961	9.6	1981	22.6
1922	6.6	1942	10.0	1962	9.4	1982	21.7
1923	7.1	1943	11.0	1963	9.6	1983	21.3
1924	7.2	1944	12.0	1964	10.0	1984	21.5
1925	7.2	1945	14.4	1965	10.6	1985	21.7
1926	7.5	1946	17.9	1966	10.9	1986	21.2
1927	7.8	1947	13.6	1967	11.2	1987	20.8
1928	7.8	1948	11.2	1968	12.4	1988	20.7
1929	8.0	1949	10.6	1969	13.4	1989	20.4
1930	7.5	1950	10.3	1970	14.9	1990	20.9
1931	7.1	1951	9.9	1971	15.7	1991	20.9
1932	6.1	1952	10.1	1972	16.9	1992	21.2
1933	6.1	1953	9.9	1973	18.2	1993	20.5
1934	7.5	1954	9.5	1974	19.3	1994	20.5
1935	7.8	1955	9.3	1975	20.3	1995	19.8
1936	8.3	1956	9.4	1976	21.1	1996	19.5
1937	8.7	1957	9.2	1977	21.1	1997	19.8
1938	8.4	1958	8.9	1978	21.9		
1939	8.5	1959	9.3	1979	22.8		

SOURCES: *Historical Statistics,* vol. 1, series B, pp. 216–20; *Vital Statistics:* 1971, pp. 2–6; *Statistical Abstract:* 1974, no. 93; 1978, no. 114; 1980, no. 124; 1982, no. 120; 1986, no. 124; 1991, no. 139; 1995, nos. 142 and 146; 1997, no. 145; National Center for Health Statistics, unpublished data.

TABLE A3-5

Marital Status of Women, Percentage Distribution, 1950–1998

Year	Divorced	Widowed	Married	Never Married	Year	Divorced	Widowed	Married	Never Married
1950	2.2	12.2	66.1	19.6	1975	5.3	13.4	66.7	14.6
1951	2.1	12.4	66.5	19.1	1976	5.7	13.1	66.2	15.0
1952	2.3	12.0	66.6	19.1	1977	6.2	12.9	65.3	15.6
1953	2.3	12.6	66.9	18.3	1978	6.7	12.7	64.2	16.4
1954	2.3	12.2	67.0	18.5	1979	6.6	13.0	63.5	16.9
1955	2.3	12.6	66.9	18.2	1980	7.1	12.8	63.0	17.1
1956	2.4	12.6	66.7	18.2	1981	7.6	12.7	62.4	17.4
1957	2.3	12.6	66.6	18.6	1982	8.0	12.5	61.9	17.6
1958	2.3	12.8	66.0	18.8	1983	7.9	12.4	61.4	18.3
1959	2.4	12.6	66.3	18.7	1984	8.3	12.5	60.8	18.4
1960	2.6	12.8	65.6	19.0	1985	8.7	12.6	60.4	18.2
1961	2.8	12.5	65.3	19.4	1986	8.9	12.4	60.5	18.3
1962	2.7	12.5	65.3	19.6	1987	8.7	12.1	60.5	18.6
1963	2.8	12.3	64.9	20.0	1988	8.8	12.1	60.4	18.7
1964	3.0	12.3	64.4	20.3	1989	9.1	12.2	59.8	18.9
1965	2.9	12.5	63.9	20.7	1990	9.3	12.1	59.7	18.9
1966	3.1	12.4	63.7	20.9	1991	9.6	11.8	59.3	19.3
1967	3.2	12.6	63.2	20.9	1992	9.9	11.7	59.1	19.2
1968	3.2	12.5	62.6	21.7	1993	10.1	11.5	59.2	19.1
1969	3.3	12.5	62.3	21.8	1994	10.2	11.2	58.8	19.7
1970	3.5	12.5	61.9	22.1	1995	10.3	11.1	59.2	19.4
1971	4.0	13.8	68.1	14.1	1996	10.5	11.0	58.6	19.9
1972	4.3	13.4	68.5	13.8	1997	11.0	10.9	57.9	20.2
1973	4.5	13.5	68.1	13.9	1998	10.8	10.8	57.9	20.5
1974	4.9	13.3	67.6	14.3					

NOTES: Data for 1950–1970 include women fourteen years old or older. Data since 1971 include women eighteen years old or older.

SOURCES: *Statistical Abstract:* 1960, no. 36; 1962, no. 32; 1963, no. 31; 1964, no. 29; 1965, no. 29; 1966, no. 32; 1967, no. 32; 1969, no. 37; 1970, no. 36; 1971, no. 38; 1972, no. 46; 1980, no. 51; 1983, no. 44; 1989, no. 50; 1990, no. 50; 1991, no. 50; 1992, no. 49; 1993, no. 49; 1994, no. 59; 1995, no. 58; 1997, no. 58; 1998, no. 61; *Historical Statistics,* series A, pp. 160–71; U.S. Bureau of the Census, unpublished tabulation.

TABLE A3-6

Births per 1,000 Unmarried Women Ages 15–44, 1940–1996

Year	Rate	Year	Rate	Year	Rate	Year	Rate
1940	7.1	1955	19.3	1970	26.4	1985	32.8
1941	7.8	1956	20.4	1971	25.6	1986	34.3
1942	8.0	1957	21.0	1972	24.9	1987	36.1
1943	8.3	1958	21.2	1973	24.5	1988	38.6
1944	9.0	1959	21.9	1974	24.1	1989	41.8
1945	10.1	1960	21.6	1975	24.5	1990	43.8
1946	10.9	1961	22.7	1976	24.3	1991	45.2
1947	12.1	1962	21.9	1977	25.6	1992	45.2
1948	12.5	1963	22.5	1978	25.7	1993	45.3
1949	13.3	1964	23.0	1979	27.2	1994	46.9
1950	14.1	1965	23.5	1980	29.4	1995	45.1
1951	15.1	1966	23.4	1981	29.6	1996	44.8
1952	15.8	1967	23.9	1982	30.0		
1953	16.9	1968	24.4	1983	30.4		
1954	18.7	1969	25.0	1984	31.0		

SOURCES: *Historical Statistics,* vol. 1, series B, pp. 28–35; *Vital Statistics:* 1972, pp. 1–30; *Statistical Abstract:* 1980, no. 95; 1987, no. 86; 1990, no. 90; 1992, no. 89; 1994, no. 100; 1995, no. 94. *Monthly Vital Statistics Report:* 1997, vol. 45, no. 11(s), table 15; 1998, vol. 46, no. 11(s), table 17; National Center for Health Statistics.

TABLE A3-7

Births per 1,000 Women Ages 15–44, 1940–1996

Year	Rate	Year	Rate	Year	Rate	Year	Rate
1940	79.9	1955	118.5	1970	87.9	1985	66.2
1941	83.4	1956	121.2	1971	81.8	1986	65.4
1942	91.5	1957	122.9	1972	73.4	1987	65.7
1943	94.3	1958	120.2	1973	69.2	1988	67.2
1944	88.8	1959	118.8	1974	68.4	1989	69.2
1945	85.9	1960	118.0	1975	66.7	1990	70.9
1946	101.9	1961	117.2	1976	65.8	1991	69.6
1947	113.3	1962	112.2	1977	67.8	1992	68.9
1948	107.3	1963	108.5	1978	66.6	1993	67.6
1949	107.1	1964	105.0	1979	68.5	1994	66.7
1950	106.2	1965	96.6	1980	68.4	1995	65.6
1951	111.5	1966	91.3	1981	67.4	1996	65.3
1952	113.9	1967	87.6	1982	68.4		
1953	115.2	1968	85.7	1983	65.8		
1954	118.1	1969	86.5	1984	65.4		

SOURCES: *Historical Statistics,* vol. 1, series B, pp. 20–27; *Statistical Abstract:* 1979, no. 83; 1980, no. 87; 1982, no. 84; 1985, no. 82; 1994, no. 92; 1995, no. 93; *Monthly Vital Statistics Report:* 1997, vol. 45, no. 11(s), table 10; 1998, vol. 46, no. 11(s), table 13; National Center for Health Statistics.

TABLE A3-8

Percentage Distribution of Families with Children under 18 by Family Head, 1950–1998

Year	Mother Only	Married Couples	Father Only	Year	Mother Only	Married Couples	Father Only
1950	6.3	92.6	1.1	1975	13.7	85.0	1.3
1951	7.8	91.1	1.1	1976	14.7	83.7	1.6
1952	7.1	91.8	1.1	1977	15.3	83.2	1.5
1953	7.0	91.7	1.3	1978	15.9	82.5	1.6
1954	7.2	91.5	1.3	1979	17.1	81.1	1.8
1955	8.1	90.8	1.1	1980	17.6	80.5	2.0
1956	7.6	91.1	1.3	1981	16.9	81.2	1.9
1957	7.6	91.3	1.1	1982	18.0	79.9	2.1
1958	7.4	91.4	1.2	1983	18.9	78.9	2.2
1959	7.8	91.3	0.9	1984	18.6	79.0	2.4
1960	8.2	90.9	0.9	1985	19.0	78.5	2.5
1961	8.4	90.9	0.7	1986	19.3	77.8	3.0
1962	8.5	90.5	1.0	1987	19.7	77.3	3.0
1963	8.3	90.4	1.3	1988	19.7	77.3	3.0
1964	8.7	90.3	1.0	1989	20.2	76.8	3.0
1965	9.2	89.9	0.9	1990	20.4	75.6	4.0
1966	9.1	89.9	1.0	1991	21.1	74.9	4.0
1967	9.4	89.4	1.2	1992	21.5	74.5	4.0
1968	9.9	89.0	1.1	1993	21.7	74.3	4.0
1969	10.2	88.7	1.1	1994	22.5	73.7	3.9
1970	10.3	88.6	1.2	1995	22.2	73.6	4.2
1971	10.2	88.6	1.2	1996	22.4	72.9	4.8
1972	11.7	87.2	1.1	1997	22.7	72.4	4.9
1973	12.2	86.6	1.2	1998	22.1	72.7	5.2
1974	12.8	85.9	1.3				

NOTE: Data for 1970 and 1980 include revisions from the Census Bureau.

SOURCE: U.S. Bureau of the Census, *Current Population Reports,* series P20-515, "Household and Family Characteristics: March 1998 (Update)," and earlier reports.

TABLE A4-1

African American and White Women's Earnings as a Percentage of Men's, 1967–1997

Year	African American	White	Year	African American	White
1967	66.9	57.9	1983	78.6	62.7
1968	65.6	58.2	1984	82.5	62.2
1969	68.2	58.1	1985	81.9	63.0
1970	69.8	58.7	1986	80.3	63.3
1971	75.2	58.5	1987	82.4	64.4
1972	70.5	56.6	1988	81.2	65.4
1973	69.6	55.9	1989	85.1	66.3
1974	75.3	57.9	1990	85.4	69.4
1975	74.6	57.6	1991	84.8	68.7
1976	75.7	59.0	1992	88.2	70.0
1977	77.5	57.6	1993	86.1	70.8
1978	71.5	58.9	1994	83.9	71.6
1979	74.6	58.8	1995	84.6	71.2
1980	78.8	58.9	1996	81.3	73.3
1981	76.0	58.5	1997	83.4	72.0
1982	78.3	60.9			

SOURCE: U.S. Census Bureau, *Historical Income Tables,* table P-33, and March *Current Population Survey.*

TABLE A4-2

Female Percentage of Total Associate's Degrees Awarded to African Americans, 1977–1996

Year	Total	Women	%	Year	Total	Women	%
1977	33,159	17,829	53.8	1991	37,657	23,939	63.6
1979	34,979	20,554	58.8	1992	39,411	25,117	63.7
1981	35,330	21,040	59.6	1993	42,340	26,843	63.4
1985	35,791	21,607	60.4	1994	45,461	28,544	62.8
1987	35,447	21,488	60.6	1995	47,142	30,356	64.4
1989	34,664	21,780	62.8	1996	50,927	33,385	65.6
1990	35,327	22,180	62.8				

NOTE: Data for 1978, 1980, 1982–1984, 1986, and 1988 are not available.

SOURCE: U.S. Department of Education, National Center for Education Statistics, Integrated Postsecondary Education Data System, "Completions" surveys, 1995–1996, and "Consolidated" survey, 1996; *Digest of Education Statistics, 1997,* table 262.

TABLE A4-3

Female Percentage of Total Bachelor's Degrees Awarded to African Americans, 1977–1996

Year	Total	Women	%	Year	Total	Women	%
1977	58,636	33,489	57.1	1991	65,341	41,013	62.8
1979	60,246	35,587	59.1	1992	72,326	45,370	62.7
1981	60,673	36,162	59.6	1993	77,872	48,989	62.9
1985	57,473	34,455	60.0	1994	83,576	52,928	63.3
1987	56,560	34,059	60.2	1995	87,203	55,428	63.6
1989	58,078	35,708	61.5	1996	89,284	57,170	64.0
1990	61,063	37,801	61.9				

NOTE: Data for 1978, 1980, 1982–1984, 1986, and 1988 are not available.

SOURCE: U.S. Department of Education, National Center for Education Statistics, Integrated Postsecondary Education Data System, "Completions" surveys, 1995–1996, and "Consolidated" survey, 1996; *Digest of Education Statistics 1997*, table 265.

TABLE A4-4

Female Percentage of Total Master's Degrees Awarded to African Americans, 1977–1996

Year	Total	Women	%	Year	Total	Women	%
1977	21,037	13,256	63.0	1991	16,139	10,430	64.6
1979	19,418	12,348	63.6	1992	18,116	12,062	66.6
1981	17,133	10,975	64.1	1993	19,780	12,959	65.5
1985	13,939	8,739	62.7	1994	21,937	14,524	66.2
1987	13,873	8,720	62.9	1995	24,171	16,068	66.5
1989	14,095	8,920	63.3	1996	24,494	16,551	67.6
1990	15,446	9,907	64.1				

NOTE: Data for 1978, 1980, 1982–1984, 1986, and 1988 are not available.

SOURCE: U.S. Department of Education, National Center for Education Statistics, Integrated Postsecondary Education Data System, "Completions" surveys, 1995–1996, and "Consolidated" survey, 1996; *Digest of Education Statistics, 1997,* table 268.

TABLE A4-5

Female Percentage of Total First Professional Degrees Awarded to African Americans, 1977–1996

Year	Total	Women	%	Year	Total	Women	%
1977	2,537	776	30.6	1991	3,575	1,903	53.2
1979	2,836	1,053	37.1	1992	3,560	1,957	55.0
1981	2,931	1,159	39.5	1993	4,100	2,323	56.7
1985	3,029	1,406	46.4	1994	4,444	2,542	57.2
1987	3,420	1,585	46.3	1995	4,747	2,670	56.2
1989	3,148	1,530	48.6	1996	4,913	2,850	58.0
1990	3,410	1,738	51.0				

NOTE: Data for 1978, 1980, 1982–1984, 1986, and 1988 are not available.

SOURCE: U.S. Department of Education, National Center for Education Statistics, Integrated Postsecondary Education Data System, "Completions" surveys, 1995–1996, and "Consolidated" survey, 1996; *Digest of Education Statistics,1997,* table 274.

TABLE A4-6

Female Percentage of Total Doctoral Degrees Awarded to African Americans, 1977–1996

Year	Total	Women	%	Year	Total	Women	%
1977	1,253	487	38.9	1991	1,211	630	52.0
1979	1,268	534	42.1	1992	1,223	647	52.9
1981	1,265	571	45.1	1993	1,352	737	54.5
1985	1,154	593	51.4	1994	1,393	762	54.7
1987	1,057	572	54.1	1995	1,667	936	56.1
1989	1,066	575	53.9	1996	1,563	867	55.5
1990	1,153	620	53.8				

NOTE: Data for 1978, 1980, 1982–1984, 1986, and 1988 are not available.

SOURCE: U.S. Department of Education, National Center for Education Statistics, Integrated Postsecondary Education Data System, "Completions" surveys, 1995–1996, and "Consolidated" survey, 1996; *Digest of Education Statistics, 1997,* table 271.

TABLE A4-7

Median Income of African American and White Women, 1948–1997

(1997 dollars)

Year	African American	White	Year	African American	White
1948	3,014	6,941	1973	8,664	9,599
1949	3,067	6,631	1974	8,702	9,639
1950	2,904	6,494	1975	8,873	9,767
1951	2,938	6,925	1976	9,181	9,743
1952	2,881	7,462	1977	8,774	10,161
1953	4,190	7,156	1978	8,814	9,789
1954	3,842	7,085	1979	8,671	9,528
1955	3,602	6,905	1980	8,932	9,648
1956	3,942	6,859	1981	8,734	9,831
1957	3,999	6,909	1982	8,836	10,018
1958	3,834	6,538	1983	8,932	10,347
1959	4,104	6,664	1984	9,522	10,735
1960	4,172	6,739	1985	9,363	10,974
1961	4,489	6,697	1986	9,615	11,364
1962	4,644	6,914	1987	9,818	12,019
1963	4,641	6,931	1988	9,971	12,350
1964	5,072	7,230	1989	10,193	12,700
1965	5,510	7,570	1990	10,227	12,669
1966	5,950	7,820	1991	10,389	12,634
1967	6,455	8,202	1992	10,167	12,541
1968	7,020	8,851	1993	10,561	12,513
1969	7,495	8,889	1994	11,419	12,595
1970	8,017	8,806	1995	11,544	12,971
1971	7,988	9,116	1996	12,042	13,258
1972	8,835	9,456	1997	13,048	13,792

SOURCE: U.S. Census Bureau, *Historical Income Tables,* table P-2, and March *Current Population Survey.*

TABLE A4-8

Percentage of Female High School Graduates in the Labor Force by Race, 1959–1998

Year	African American	White		Year	African American	White
1959	30.0	59.7		1978	63.5	77.6
1962	37.6	62.7		1979	65.8	78.7
1964	39.7	64.1		1980	68.3	80.3
1965	42.7	65.2		1981	70.0	81.1
1966	43.7	66.8		1982	70.8	82.0
1967	45.9	67.5		1983	74.7	83.0
1968	48.0	69.2		1984	75.7	83.9
1969	49.0	70.6		1990	82.7	89.1
1970	52.9	71.8		1991	83.1	89.6
1971	55.2	72.9		1992	83.8	90.3
1972	54.8	71.3		1993	86.0	91.0
1973	58.7	72.7		1994	87.4	91.8
1974	60.2	74.0		1995	87.8	92.0
1975	62.3	74.9		1996	88.6	91.8
1976	64.6	76.1		1997	87.7	91.9
1977	62.3	76.8		1998	87.8	92.0

NOTE: Data for 1960, 1961, 1963, and 1985–1989 are not available.

SOURCES: *Handbook of Labor Statistics,* 1985, table 61; Bureau of Labor Statistics, unpublished data from the *Current Population Survey,* annual averages, 1990–1998.

Bibliography

Abrams, Kathryn. "Gender Discrimination and the Transformation of Workplace Norms." *Vanderbilt Law Review* 42 (1989): 1183–248.

———. "The Reasonable Woman: Sense and Sensibility in Sexual Harassment Law." *Dissent* 42 (Winter 1995): 48–54.

———. "Social Construction, Roving Biologism, and Reasonable Women: A Response to Professor Epstein." *DePaul Law Review* 41 (1992): 1021–40.

Adler, Robert S., and Ellen R. Peirce. "The Legal, Ethical, and Social Implications of the 'Reasonable Woman' Standard in Sexual Harassment Cases." *Fordham Law Review* 61: 773–827.

Arbery, Walter Christopher. "A Step Backward for Equality Principles: The 'Reasonable Woman' Standard in Title VII Hostile Work Environment Sexual Harassment Claims." *Georgia Law Review* 27 (1993): 503–53.

Aronberg, David. "Crumbling Foundations: Why Recent Judicial and Legislative Challenges to Title IX May Signal Its Demise." *Florida Law Review* 47 (1995): 741–813.

Barrett, Nancy Smith. "Comments." Commentary on "The Persistence of Male-Female Earnings Differentials" by Ronald L. Oaxaca. In F. Thomas Juster, ed., *The Distribution of Economic Well-Being.* Cambridge: Ballinger Publishing Company (for National Bureau of Economic Research), 1977: 344–51.

Becker, Gary S. *Human Capital: A Theoretical and Empirical Analysis, with Special Reference to Education,* 2d ed. New York: Columbia University Press (for National Bureau of Economic Research), 1975.

Beer, William R. "Resolute Ignorance: Social Science and Affirmative Action." *Society* 24 (May/June 1987): 63–69.

Beller, Andrea H. "The Impact of Equal Employment Opportunity Laws on the Male-Female Earnings Differential." In Cynthia B. Lloyd, Emily S. Andrews, and Curtis L. Gilroy, eds., *Women in the Labor Market.* New York: Columbia University Press, 1979, 305–30.

———. "Occupational Segregation by Sex: Determinants and Changes," *Journal of Human Resources* 17 (Summer 1982): 371–92.

Benokraitis, Nijole V., and Joe R. Feagin. *Modern Sexism: Blatant, Subtle, and Covert Discrimination,* 2d ed. Englewood Cliffs, N.J.: Prentice-Hall, 1994.

Blau, Francine D. "Gender and Economic Outcomes: The Role of Wage Structure." *Labour* 7 (1) (1993): 73–92.

———. "Occupational Segregation and Labor Market Discrimination." In Barbara F. Reskin, ed., *Sex Segregation and the Workplace: Trends, Explanations, Remedies.* Washington, D.C.: National Academy Press, 1984.

———. "Trends in the Well-Being of American Women, 1970–1995." *Journal of Economic Literature* 36 (1998): 112–65.

———. "Women's Work, Women's Lives: A Comparative Economic Perspective." NBER Working Paper Series no. 3447, National Bureau of Economic Research, September 1990.

Blau, Francine D., and Andrea H. Beller. "Trends in Earnings Differentials by Gender, 1971–1981." *Industrial and Labor Relations Review* 41 (1988): 513–29.

Blau, Francine D., and Marianne A. Ferber. "Women's Work, Women's Lives: A Comparative Economic Perspective." In Hilda Kahne and Janet Z. Giele, eds., *Women's Work and Women's Lives: The Continuing Struggle Worldwide.* Boulder, Colo.: Westview Press, 1992, 28–44.

Blau, Francine D., and Lawrence M. Kahn. "The Gender Earnings Gap: Learning from International Comparisons." *American Economic Review Papers and Proceedings* 82 (1992): 533–38.

———. "The Gender Earnings Gap: Some International Evidence." NBER Working Paper Series no. 4224, National Bureau of Economic Research, December 1992.

———. "The Impact of Wage Structure on Trends in U.S. Gender Wage Differentials: 1975–87." NBER Working Paper Series no. 4748, National Bureau of Economic Research, May 1994.

———. "Race and Gender Pay Differentials." NBER Working Paper Series no. 4120, National Bureau of Economic Research, July 1992.

———. "Race and Gender Pay Differentials." In David Lewin, Olivia S. Mitchell, and Peter D. Sherer, eds., *Research Frontiers in Industrial Relations and Human Resources.* Madison, Wisc.: Industrial Relations Research Association, 1992, 381–416.

———. "Rising Wage Inequality and the U.S. Gender Gap." *American Economic Review Papers and Proceedings* 84 (1994): 23–28.

———. "Swimming Upstream: Trends in the Gender Wage Differential in the 1980s." *Journal of Labor Economics* 15 (1997): 1–42.

———. "Wage Structure and Gender Earnings Differentials: An International Comparison." *Economica* 63 (May 1996), S29–S62.

Bowman, Karlyn. "The Gender Factor." In Everett Carll Ladd, ed., *America at the Polls 1994.* Storrs, Conn.: Roper Center for Public Opinion Research, 1995, 52–57.

Brown, Charles, and Mary Corcoran. "Sex-Based Differences in School Content and the Male/Female Wage Gap." *Journal of Labor Economics* 15 (3), pt. 1, July 1997, 431–65.

Browne, Kingsley R. "Sex and Temperament in Modern Society: A Darwinian View of the Glass Ceiling and the Gender Gap." *Arizona Law Review* 37 (1995): 971–1106.

Carvin, Michael. "Disparate Impact Claims under the New Title VII." *Notre Dame Law Review* 68 (1993), 1153–64.

Catalyst. *The 1998 Catalyst Census of Women Corporate Officers and Top Earners.* New York: Catalyst, November 1998.

Center for the American Woman and Politics, Eagleton Institute of Politics, Rutgers University. "Women in the U.S. Congress 1996." Fact sheet. New Brunswick, N.J.: Center for the American Woman and Politics, 1995.

Connelly, Marjorie. "A Look at Voting Patterns of 115 Demographic Groups in House Races." *New York Times,* November 9, 1998, p. A20.

Corcoran, Mary, and Greg J. Duncan. "Work History, Labor Force Attachment, and Earnings Differences between the Races and Sexes." *Journal of Human Resources* 14 (1979): 3–20.

Costa, Dora L. "The Unequal Work Day: A Long-Term View." NBER Working Paper Series no. 6419, National Bureau of Economic Research, February 1998.

———. "The Wage and the Length of the Work Day: From the 1890s to 1991." NBER Working Paper Series no. 6504, National Bureau of Economic Research, April 1998.

Costello, Cynthia, and Barbara Kivimae Krimgold, eds. *The American Woman, 1996–97.* New York: W. W. Norton & Company, 1996.

Crittenden, Danielle. *What Our Mothers Didn't Tell Us: Why Happiness Eludes the Modern Woman.* New York: Simon and Schuster, 1999.

Davidson, Marilyn J., and Cary L. Cooper. *Shattering the Glass Ceiling.* London: Paul Chapman, 1992.

DeWitt, Karen. "Feminists Gather to Affirm the Relevancy of Their Movement." *New York Times,* February 3, 1996, A9.

Diebold, Francis X., David Neumark, and Daniel Polsky. "Job Stability in the United States." *Journal of Labor Economics* 15 (1997): 206–33.

Donohue, John J., III. "Diverting the Coasean River: Incentive Schemes to Reduce Unemployment Spells." *Yale Law Journal* 99 (1989): 549–609.

———. "Employment Discrimination Law in Perspective: Three Concepts of Equality." *Michigan Law Review* 92 (1994): 2583–612.

———. "Further Thoughts on Employment Discrimination Legislation: A Reply to Judge Posner." *University of Pennsylvania Law Review* 136 (1987): 523–51.

———. "The Impact of Federal Civil Rights Policy on the Economic Status of Blacks." *Harvard Journal of Law and Public Policy* 14 (1991): 41–52.

———. "Is Title VII Efficient?" *University of Pennsylvania Law Review* 134 (1986): 1411–31.

———. "Prohibiting Sex Discrimination in the Workplace: An Economic Perspective." *University of Chicago Law Review* 56 (1989): 1337–68.

Donohue, John J., III, and James Heckman. "Continuous versus Episodic Change: The Impact of Civil Rights Policy on the Economic Status of Blacks." *Journal of Economic Literature* 29 (1991): 1603–43.

———. "Re-Evaluating Federal Civil Rights Policy." *Georgetown Law Journal* 79 (1991): 1713–35.

Donohue, John J., III, and Peter Siegelman. "The Changing Nature of Employment Discrimination Litigation." *Stanford Law Review* 43 (1991): 983–1033.

———. "Law and Macroeconomics: Employment Discrimination Litigation over the Business Cycle." *Southern California Law Review* 66 (1993): 709–65.

Dowd, Nancy E. "Liberty vs. Equality: In Defense of Privileged White Males." *William and Mary Law Review* 34 (1993): 429–85.

———. "Work and Family: The Gender Paradox and the Limitations of Discrimination Analysis in Restructuring the Workplace." *Harvard Civil Rights–Civil Liberties Law Review* 24 (1989): 79–172.

England, Paula. *Comparable Worth: Theories and Evidence.* Hawthorne, N.Y.: Aldine de Gruyter, 1992.

England, Paula, George Farkas, Barbara Stanek Kilbourne, and Thomas Dou. "Explaining Occupational Sex Segregation and Wages: Findings from a Model with Fixed Effects." *American Sociological Review* 53 (1988): 544–58.

England, Paula, Lori L. Reid, and Barbara Stanek Kilbourne. "The Effect of the Sex Composition of Jobs on Starting Wages in an Organization: Findings from the NLSY." *Demography* 33 (1996): 511–21.

Epstein, Richard A. "The Authoritarian Impulse in Sex Discrimination Law: A Reply to Professors Abrams and Strauss." *DePaul Law Review* 41 (1992): 1041–56.

———. "Gender Is for Nouns." *DePaul Law Review* 41 (1992): 981–1005.

———. "Two Conceptions of Civil Rights." *Social Philosophy and Policy* 8 (2) (1991): 38–59.

———. "The Varieties of Self-Interest." *Social Philosophy and Policy* 8 (1) (1990): 102–20.

Even, William E., and David A. Macpherson. "The Decline of Private-Sector Unionism and the Gender Wage Gap." *Journal of Human Resources* 28 (1993): 279–96.

Feminist Majority Foundation. "U.S. Supreme Court Rejects Challenge to California Affirmative Action Ban." *Feminist Majority Report* 9 (1997): 3.

Fields, Judith, and Edward N. Wolff. "The Decline of Sex Segregation and the Wage Gap, 1970–80." *Journal of Human Resources* 26 (1991): 608–22.

Finley, Lucinda M. "Transcending Equality Theory: A Way Out of the Maternity and Workplace Debate." *Columbia Law Review* 86 (1986): 1118–82.

Fox-Genovese, Elizabeth. *Feminism Is Not the Story of My Life.* New York: Doubleday, 1996.

———. *Feminism without Illusions: A Critique of Individualism.* Chapel Hill: University of North Carolina Press, 1991.

Fuchs, Victor A. *Women's Quest for Economic Equality.* Cambridge: Harvard University Press, 1988.

Gibbons, Robert, and Lawrence F. Katz. "Does Unmeasured Ability Explain Interindustry Wage Differentials?" *Review of Economic Studies* 59 (1992): 515–35.

Glass Ceiling Commission. *Good for Business: Making Full Use of the Nation's Human Capital.* Washington, D.C.: Government Printing Office, March 1995.

Goldin, Claudia. "Career and Family: College Women Look to the Past." In Francine Blau and Ronald Ehrenberg, eds., *Gender and Family Issues in the Workplace.* New York: Russell Sage Foundation, 1997.

———. "Life Cycle Labor Force Participation of Married Women: Historical Evidence and Implications." *Journal of Labor Economics* 7 (1989): 20–47.

———. *Understanding the Gender Gap.* New York: Oxford University Press, 1990.

Gramm, Wendy Lee. "Household Utility Maximization and the Working Wife." *American Economic Review* 65 (1975): 90–100.

Gronau, Reuben. "The Theory of Home Production: The Past Ten Years." *Journal of Labor Economics* 15 (1997): 197–205.

Groshen, Erica L. "The Structure of the Female/Male Wage Differential: Is It Who You Are, What You Do, or Where You Work?" *Journal of Human Resources* 26 (1991): 457–72.

Gross, Martin L. *The End of Sanity: Social and Cultural Madness in America.* New York: Avon Books, 1997.

Gruber, Jonathan. "Health Insurance and the Labor Market." Working paper, Department of Economics, Massachusetts Institute of Technology, August 1998.

———. "The Incidence of Payroll Taxation: Evidence from Chile." *Journal of Labor Economics* 15 (3), pt. 2 (1997): S72–S101.

Gruber, Jonathan, and Alan B. Krueger. "The Incidence of Mandated Employer-Provided Insurance: Lessons from Workers' Compensation Insurance." In David Bradford, ed., *Tax Policy and the Economy.* Cambridge: National Bureau of Economic Research and MIT Press, 1991, 111–43.

Gupta, Nabanita Datta. "Probabilities of Job Choice and Employer Selection and Male-Female Occupational Differences." *American Economic Review Papers and Proceedings* 83 (1993): 57–61.

Hamermesh, Daniel S. "Immigration and the Quality of Jobs." NBER Working Paper Series no. 6195, National Bureau of Economic Research, September 1997.

Hellerstein, Judith K., and David Neumark. "Are Earnings Profiles Steeper than Productivity Profiles? Evidence from Israeli Firm-Level Data." *Journal of Human Resources* 30 (1993): 89–112.

Hellerstein, Judith K., David Neumark, and Kenneth R. Troske. "Wages, Productivity, and Worker Characteristics: Evidence from Plant-Level Production Functions and Wage Equations." NBER Working Paper Series no. 5626, National Bureau of Economic Research, June 1996.

Hersch, Joni. "Equal Employment Opportunity Law and Firm Profitability." *Journal of Human Resources* 26 (1989): 139–53.

Hill, M. Anne, and June E. O'Neill. "Intercohort Change in Women's Labor Market Status." In Ronald G. Ehrenberg, ed., *Research in Labor Economics.* Greenwich, Conn.: JAI Press, 1992.

Hochschild, Arlie Russell. *The Time Bind: When Work Becomes Home and Home Becomes Work.* New York: Henry Holt & Company, 1997.

Hunt, Jennifer. "The Transition in East Germany: When Is a Ten-Point Fall in the Gender Wage Gap Bad News?" NBER Working Paper Series no. 6167, National Bureau of Economic Research, September 1997.

Institute for Women's Policy Research. *The Status of Women in the States, Second Edition, 1998–1999.* Washington, D.C.: Institute for Women's Policy Research, October 1998.

Ippolito, Richard A. "A Study of Wages and Reliability." *Journal of Law and Economics* 39 (1996): 149–89.

Johnson, George, and Gary Solon. "Estimates of the Direct Effects of Comparable Worth Policy." *American Economic Review* 76 (1986): 1117–25.

Juhn, Chinhui, and Kevin M. Murphy. "Wage Inequality and Family Labor Supply." *Journal of Labor Economics* 15 (1997): 72–97.

Klepinger, Daniel, Shelly Lundberg, and Robert Plotnick. "How Does the Adolescent Fertility Act Affect the Human Capital and Wages of Young Women?" Institute for Research on Poverty Discussion Paper no. 1145-97, September 1997.

Kolpin, Van W., and Larry D. Singell, Jr. "The Gender Composition and Scholarly Performance of Economics Departments: A Test for Employment Discrimination." *Industrial and Labor Relations Review* 49 (1996): 408–23.

Korenman, Sanders, and David Neumark. "Does Marriage Really Make Men More Productive?" *Journal of Human Resources* 26 (1991): 282–307.

———. "Marriage, Motherhood, and Wages." *Journal of Human Resources* 27 (1992): 233–35.

Korn/Ferry. *Korn/Ferry International's 25th Annual Board of Directors Study.* New York: Korn/Ferry, April 1998.

Kossoudji, Sherri A., and Laura J. Dresser. "Working Class Rosies: Women Industrial Workers during World War II." *Journal of Economic History* 52 (1992): 431–46.

Kosters, Marvin. *Wage Levels and Inequality: Measuring and Interpreting the Trends.* Washington, D.C.: AEI Press, 1998.

———. "Wages and Demographics." In Marvin Kosters, ed., *Workers and Their Wages: Changing Patterns in the United States.* Washington, D.C.: AEI Press, 1991, 1–32.

Krantz, Les. *The Jobs Rated Almanac,* rev. ed. New York: World Almanac, 1992.

Kristol, Irving. "Sex Trumps Gender." *Wall Street Journal,* March 6, 1996.

Lazear, Edward. "Male-Female Wage Differentials: Has the Government Had Any Effect?" In Cynthia B. Lloyd, Emily S. Andrews, and Curtis L. Gilroy, *Women in the Labor Market.* New York: Columbia University Press, 1979, 331–51.

Leonard, Jonathan S. "The Impact of Affirmative Action Regulation and Equal Employment Law on Black Employment." *Journal of Economic Perspectives* 4 (Fall 1990): 47–63.

Lewenhak, Sheila. *The Revaluation of Women's Work.* London: Earthscan, 1992.

Lundberg, Shelly J., and Richard Starz. "Private Discrimination and Social Intervention in Competitive Labor Markets." *American Economic Review* 73 (1983): 340–47.

Lynch, Frederick R. *Invisible Victims: White Males and the Crisis of Affirmative Action.* Westport, Conn.: Greenwood Press, 1989.

Lynch, Michael, and Katherine Post. "What Glass Ceiling?" *The Public Interest,* no. 124 (Summer 1996): 27–36.

Macpherson, David A., and Barry T. Hirsch. "Wages and Gender Composition: Why Do Women's Jobs Pay Less?" *Journal of Labor Economics* 13 (1995): 426–71.

Marshall, Judi. *Women Managers Moving On.* New York: Routledge, 1995.

McCormick, Katheryne, and Lytisha Williams. "Gender Gap a Factor in a Majority of Races in 1994." *News and Notes*, Center for the American Woman and Politics, Winter 1994, 7–8.

McKeown, James T. "Statistics for Wage Discrimination Cases: Why the Statistical Models Used Cannot Prove or Disprove Sex Discrimination." *Indiana Law Journal* 67 (1992): 633–61.

McMillen, Daniel P., and Larry D. Singell, Jr. "Gender Differences in First Jobs for Economists." *Southern Economic Journal* 60 (1994): 701–14.

Michael, Robert T., Heidi I. Hartmann, and Brigid O'Farrell, eds. *Pay Equity: Empirical Inquiries*. Washington, D.C.: National Academy Press, 1989.

Mickens, Alvin. "Comments." Commentary on "The Persistence of Male-Female Earnings Differentials" by Ronald L. Oaxaca. In F. Thomas Juster, ed., *The Distribution of Economic Well-Being*. Cambridge: Ballinger Publishing Company (for National Bureau of Economic Research), 1977, 352–54.

Mincer, Jacob. "Labor Force Participation of Married Women: A Study of Labor Supply." In C. Christ, ed., *Aspects of Labor Economics*. Princeton: Princeton University Press, 1962.

———. "On the Job Training: Costs, Returns, and Some Implications." *Journal of Political Economy* (October 1962): 50–59.

———. *Schooling, Experience, and Earnings*. New York: Columbia University Press (for the National Bureau of Economic Research), 1974.

Mincer, Jacob, and Haim Ofek. "Interrupted Work Careers: Depreciation and Restoration of Human Capital." *Journal of Human Resources* 17 (1982): 3–24.

Mincer, Jacob, and Solomon Polachek. "Family Investments in Human Capital: Earnings of Women." *Journal of Political Economy* 82 (March–April 1974): S76–S108.

Moore, Dorothy P., and E. Holly Buttner. *Women Entrepreneurs: Moving beyond the Glass Ceiling*. Thousand Oaks, Calif.: Sage Publications, Inc., 1997.

Morrison, Ann M. *Breaking the Glass Ceiling: Can Women Reach the Top of America's Largest Corporations?* New York: Addison-Wesley, 1987.

Murphy, Kevin M., and Finis Welch. "The Role of International Trade in Wage Differentials." In Marvin Kosters, ed., *Workers and Their Wages: Changing Patterns in the United States*. Washington, D.C.: AEI Press, 1991, 39–69.

Nager, Glen D. "Affirmative Action after the Civil Rights Act of 1991: The Effects of a 'Neutral' Statute." *Notre Dame Law Review* 68 (1993): 1057–94.

National Foundation of Women Business Owners, Catalyst, and The Committee of 200. *Paths to Entrepreneurship: New Directions for Women in Business*. February 1998.

National Organization for Women. "NOW Targets Smith Barney as First 'Merchant of Shame'; Calls All Employers to Take Women-Friendly Workplace Pledge." Press release. Washington, D.C.: National Organization for Women, March 12, 1997.

Nelson, Julie A. "Feminism and Economics." *Journal of Economic Perspectives* 9 (Spring 1995): 131–48.

———. *Feminism, Objectivity, and Economics.* London: Routledge, 1996.

Neumark, David. "Labor Market Information and Wage Differentials by Race and Sex." NBER Working Paper Series no. 6573, National Bureau of Economic Research, May 1998.

Neumark, David, and Sanders Korenman. "Sources of Bias in Women's Wage Equations: Results Using Sibling Data." *Journal of Human Resources* 29 (1994): 379–405.

Neumark, David, and Michele McLennan. "Sex Discrimination and Women's Labor Market Outcomes." *Journal of Human Resources* 30 (1994): 713–40.

Newman, Jody. "The Gender Story: Women as Voters and Candidates in the 1996 Elections." In Regina Dougherty, Everett C. Ladd, David Wilber, and Lynn Zayachkiwsky, eds., *America at the Polls 1996.* Storrs, Conn.: Roper Center for Public Opinion Research, 1997.

Nivola, Pietro S., ed. *Comparative Disadvantages? Social Regulations and the Global Economy.* Washington, D.C.: Brookings Institution Press, 1997.

Nossel, Suzanne, and Elizabeth Westfall. *Presumed Equal: What America's Top Women Lawyers Really Think about Their Firms.* Franklin Lakes, N.J.: Career Press, 1998.

Oaxaca, Ronald L. "The Persistence of Male-Female Earnings Differentials." In F. Thomas Juster, ed., *The Distribution of Economic Well-Being.* Cambridge: Ballinger Publishing Company (for National Bureau of Economic Research), 1977, 303–54.

Oaxaca, Ronald L., and Michael R. Ransom. "On Discrimination and the Decomposition of Wage Differentials." *Journal of Econometrics* 61 (1994): 5–21.

O'Brien, Virginia. *Success on Our Own Terms: Tales of Extraordinary, Ordinary Business Women.* New York: John Wiley & Sons, 1998.

Ogawa, Naohiro, and John F. Ermisch. "Family Structure, Home Time Demands, and the Employment Patterns of Japanese Married Women." *Journal of Labor Economics* 14 (1996): 677–702.

O'Melveny, Mary K. "Playing the 'Gender' Card: Affirmative Action and Working Women." *Kentucky Law Journal* 84 (1996): 863–901.

O'Neill, Dave M., and June O'Neill. "Affirmative Action in the Labor Market." *Annals of the American Academy of Political and Social Science* 523 (September 1992): 88–103.

O'Neill, June. "The Causes and Significance of the Declining Gender Gap." Talk given at Bard College, September 22, 1994.

———. "Comparable Worth." In David R. Henderson, ed., *Fortune Encyclopedia of Economics.* New York: Warner Books, 1993.

———. "Comparable Worth: A Symposium on the Issues." Washington, D.C.: Equal Employment Advisory Council, 1982.

———. "The Determinants and Wage Effects of Occupational Segregation." Working paper. Washington, D.C.: Urban Institute, March 1983.

———. "Discrimination and Income Differences." In Susan Feiner, ed., *Race and Gender in the American Economy.* Englewood Cliffs, N.J.: Prentice-Hall, 1994.

————. "A Report on the Salaries of Economists." Prepared for the American Economic Association, Commission on Graduate Education in Economics, January 1990.

————. "The Shrinking Pay Gap." *Wall Street Journal,* October 7, 1994, A10.

————. "The Trend in the Male-Female Wage Gap in the United States." *Journal of Labor Economics* 3 (January 1985): S91–S116.

O'Neill, June, and Solomon Polachek. "Why the Gender Gap in Wages Narrowed in the 1980s." *Journal of Labor Economics* 11 (1993): 205–29.

Orlans, Harold, and June O'Neill. "Preface." *Annals of the American Academy of Political and Social Science* 523 (September 1992): 7–9.

Oster, Sharon M. "Is There a Policy Problem? The Gender Wage Gap." *Georgetown Law Journal* 82 (1993): 109–19.

Paul, Ellen Frankel. "Sexual Harassment as Sex Discrimination: A Defective Paradigm." *Yale Law and Policy Review* 8 (1990): 333–65.

Phelps, Edmund S. "The Statistical Theory of Racism and Sexism." *American Economic Review* 62 (1972): 659–61.

Phillips, Michael M. "Winning Streak: As Economy Thrives, So Do Many Workers Accustomed to Poverty." *Wall Street Journal*, March 4, 1998, A1.

Polachek, Solomon W. "Differences in Expected Postschool Investment as a Determinant of Market Wage Differentials." *International Economic Review* 16 (1975): 451–69.

————. "Occupational Segregation among Women: Theory, Evidence, and a Prognosis." In Cynthia B. Lloyd, Emily Andrews, and Curtis Gilroy, eds., *Women in the Labor Market.* New York: Columbia University Press, 1979.

Polachek, Solomon, and C. Kao. "Lifetime Labor Force Expectations in the Male-Female Earnings Gap." In R. Cornwell and P. Wunnava, eds., *New Approaches to the Analysis of Discrimination.* New York: Praeger, 1991, 199–238.

Posner, Richard A. "An Economic Analysis of Sex Discrimination Laws." *University of Chicago Law Review* 56 (1989): 1311–35.

————. "The Efficiency and the Efficacy of Title VII." *University of Pennsylvania Law Review* 136 (1987): 417–521.

Povall, Margery. "Positive Action for Women in Britain." *Annals of the American Academy of Political and Social Science* 523 (September 1992): 175–85.

Powers, Elizabeth. "A Farewell to Feminism." *Commentary*, January 1997, 23–30.

Rhode, Deborah. *Speaking of Sex: The Denial of Gender Inequality.* Cambridge: Harvard University Press, 1997.

Richardson, Valerie. "Women Take Over in Arizona; Will Enter State's Top Five Offices." *Washington Times*, December 30, 1998, A1, A18.

Riggs, B. L., and L. J. Melton III. "The Prevention and Treatment of Osteoporosis." *New England Journal of Medicine* 327 (1992): 620–27.

Robinson, John P., and Geoffrey Godbey. *Time for Life: The Surprising Ways Americans Use Their Time.* University Park, Penn.: Pennsylvania State University Press, 1997.

Rodgers, William M., III, and William E. Spriggs. "The Effect of Federal Contractor Status on Racial Differences in Establishment-Level Employment Shares: 1979–1992." *American Economic Review Papers and Proceedings* 86 (1996): 290–93.

Roper Starch Worldwide Survey. Cited in "Women and Work." *The American Enterprise*, March/April 1996, 91.

Rotunda, Ronald D. "The Civil Rights Act of 1991: A Brief Introductory Analysis of the Congressional Response to Judicial Interpretation." *Notre Dame Law Review* 68 (1993): 923–53.

Ruhm, Christopher J. "The Economic Consequences of Parental Leave Mandates: Lessons from Europe." NBER Working Paper Series no. 5688, National Bureau of Economic Research, July 1996.

———. "Parental Leave and Child Health." NBER Working Paper Series no. 6554, National Bureau of Economic Research, May 1998.

Ruhm, Christopher J., and Jackqueline L. Teague. "Parental Leave Policies in Europe and North America." NBER Working Paper Series no. 5065, National Bureau of Economic Research, March 1995.

Saffer, Henry, and Frank Chaloupka. "Demographic Differentials in the Demand for Alcohol and Illicit Drugs." NBER Working Paper Series no. 6432, National Bureau of Economic Research, February 1998.

Sawhill, Isabel V. "Comment." In Cynthia B. Lloyd, Emily S. Andrews, and Curtis L. Gilroy, eds., *Women in the Labor Market.* New York: Columbia University Press, 1979, 352–55.

Schnapper, Eric. "Statutory Misinterpretations: A Legal Autopsy." *Notre Dame Law Review* 68 (1993): 1095–1152.

Schultz, Vicki. "Telling Stories about Women and Work: Judicial Interpretations of Sex Segregation in the Workplace in Title VII Cases Raising the Lack of Interest Argument." *Harvard Law Review* 103 (1990): 1749–1843.

Siegelman, Peter, and John J. Donohue III. "The Selection of Employment Discrimination Disputes for Litigation: Using Business-Cycle Effects to Test the Priest-Klein Hypothesis." *Journal of Legal Studies* 24 (1995): 427–62.

Simon, Rita J., ed. *From Data to Public Policy: Affirmative Action, Domestic Violence, and Social Welfare.* Lanham, Md.: Women's Freedom Network and University Press of America, 1996.

———. *Neither Victim nor Enemy: Women's Freedom Network Looks at Gender in America.* Lanham, Md.: Women's Freedom Network and University Press of America, 1995.

Singell, Larry D., Jr., and Joe A. Stone. "Gender Differences in Ph.D. Economists' Careers." *Contemporary Policy Issues* 4 (October 1993): 95–106.

Singell, Larry D., Jr., and James Thornton. "Nepotism, Discrimination, and the Persistence of Utility-Maximizing, Owner-Operated Firms." *Southern Economic Journal* 63 (1997): 904–19.

Smith, James P., and Michael Ward. "Women in the Labor Market and in the Family." *Journal of Economic Perspectives* 3 (Winter 1989): 9–23.

————. "Women's Wages and Work in the Twentieth Century." Santa Monica: RAND Corporation, 1984.

Sneirson, Amy M. "One of These Things Is Not Like the Other: Proving Liability under the Equal Pay Act and Title VII." *Washington University Law Quarterly* 72 (1994): 783–95.

Sommers, Christina Hoff. *Who Stole Feminism?* New York: Simon and Schuster, 1994.

Soreson, Elaine. *Comparable Worth: Is It a Worthy Policy?* Princeton: Princeton University Press, 1994.

————. *Exploring the Reasons Behind the Narrowing Gender Gap in Earnings.* Washington, D.C.: Urban Institute, 1991.

Sowell, Thomas. *Preferential Policies: An International Perspective.* New York: William Morrow and Company, Inc., 1990.

Steinem, Gloria. "Revving Up for the Next 25 Years." *Ms.,* September/October 1997, 82.

Strauss, David A. "Biology, Difference, and Gender Discrimination." *DePaul Law Review* 41 (1992): 1007–20.

Strossen, Nadine. "Women's Rights under Siege." *North Dakota Law Review* 73 (1997): 207–30.

Suen, Wing. "Decomposing Wage Residuals: Unmeasured Skill or Statistical Artifact?" *Journal of Labor Economics* 15 (3), pt. 1 (1997): 555–66.

Sunstein, Cass R. "Why Markets Don't Stop Discrimination." *Social Philosophy and Policy* 8 (2) (1990–1991): 22–37.

Symposium: "Is Affirmative Action on the Way Out? Should It Be?" *Commentary* 105 (March 1998): 18–57.

Thernstrom, Stephan, and Abigail Thernstrom. "The Consequences of Colorblindness." *Wall Street Journal*, April 7, 1998, A18.

Tobias, Sheila. *Faces of Feminism: An Activist's Reflections on the Women's Movement.* Boulder, Colo.: Westview Press, 1997.

Tomasson, Richard F., Faye J. Crosby, and Sharon D. Herzberger. *Affirmative Action: The Pros and Cons of Policy and Practice.* Washington, D.C.: American University Press, 1996.

U.S. Bureau of the Census, *Current Population Reports*, Series P-20-482. Washington, D.C.: Government Printing Office, 1995.

U.S. Department of Education. *Digest of Education Statistics, 1997.* Washington, D.C.: Government Printing Office, 1997.

U.S. Department of Labor, Bureau of Labor Statistics. *Census of Fatal Occupational Injuries, 1997.* Washington, D.C.: Government Printing Office, August 1998.

————. *Survey of Occupational Injuries and Illnesses, 1996.* Washington, D.C.: Government Printing Office, April 1998.

U.S. House Committee on Government Operations. *Failure and Fraud in Civil Rights Enforcement by the Department of Education.* Report 100-334. 100th Congress, 1st Session, October 2, 1987.

U.S. House Subcommittee on Commerce, Consumer Protection, and Competitiveness. *Gender Equity Regulation of Title IX and the Involvement of Women in College Sports.* Serial no. 103-1. 103d Congress, 1st Session, February 17, 1993.

U.S. House Subcommittee on Postsecondary Education, Training, and Life-Long Learning. *Hearing on Title IX of the Education Amendments of 1972.* 104th Congress, 1st Session, May 9, 1995.

U.S. Small Business Administration, Office of Advocacy. *Women in Business.* Washington, D.C.: Government Printing Office, October 1998.

Waldfogel, Jane. "The Family Gap for Young Women in the United States and Britain: Can Maternity Leave Make a Difference?" *Journal of Labor Economics* 16 (1998): 505–45.

———. "Working Mothers Then and Now: A Cross-Cohort Analysis of the Effects of Maternity Leave on Women's Pay." In Francine D. Blau and Ronald G. Ehrenberg, eds., *Gender and Family Issues in the Workplace.* New York: Russell Sage Foundation, 1997.

Wallace, Geoffrey, and Rebecca M. Blank. "What Goes Up Must Come Down? Explaining Recent Changes in Public Assistance Caseloads." Paper prepared for the conference Welfare Reform and the Macro Economy sponsored by the Joint Center on Poverty Research, October 1998.

Wallace, Phyllis A. "Comment." In Cynthia B. Lloyd, Emily S. Andrews, and Curtis L. Gilroy, eds., *Women in the Labor Market.* New York: Columbia University Press, 1979, 356–61.

White, Barbara, Charles Cox, and Cary Cooper. *Women's Career Development: A Study of High Flyers.* Cambridge: Blackwell, 1993.

Wood, Robert G., Mary E. Corcoran, and Paul N. Courant. "Pay Differences among the Highly Paid: The Male-Female Earnings Gap in Lawyers' Salaries." *Journal of Labor Economics* 11 (1993): 417–41.

Zank, Neal S. *Measuring the Employment Effects of Regulation: Where Did the Jobs Go?* Westport, Conn.: Quorum Books, 1996.

Index

Affirmative action, 74
African American women, 65–70
    and voting, 44
Aid to Families with Dependent
    Children, 59

Becker, Mary, 34
Beller, Andrea H., 36
Birth rate, 56, 57
Blank, Rebecca, 59–60
Bowman, Karlyn, 43
Browne, Kingsley, 33
Business world, women in, xx–xxi,
    37–38

Candidates for state elected officials, 41
Catalyst, 13
Center for the American Woman and
    Politics, 39, 43
Child-rearing responsibilities, 12–13,
    17–18, 58
Children, as factor in women's
    earnings, 14–15
Choices, personal
    family or job, 18
    implications for earnings, 12
    occupational, 33–36
    significance of for women, 79–80
Civil Rights Act
    of 1964, 79
    of 1991, 18
Congress, women in, 39–43
Connelly, Marjorie, 48
Corporate boards, women on, 19
Crittenden, Danielle, 66n3
Crosby, Faye J., 6n2

Death rates on the job, 33–35
Degrees, awarded to African
    American women
    associate's, 66
    bachelor's, 67
    doctoral, 69
    first professional, 68
    master's, 67
Degrees, awarded to women, 22
    associate's, 23
    bachelor's, 23
    dentistry, 26
    doctoral, 24
    first professional, 25
    law, 26
    master's, 24
    master's in business, 25
    medical, 27
DeWitt, Karen, 6n2
Discrimination, 4
    evaluating claims of, 73–76
    explanations of, 5
    as factor in preventing women's
        advancement, 20
    forces "pink ghetto," 33
    standards of evidence for, 74–76
    against women with children, 16
Divorce, 54, 55

Earnings
    differences between African
        American and white women,
        66, 68, 69
    ratio of women's to men's, 14–15
    See also Wage gap

Economy, impact on discrimination, 4, 73
Education
    as factor in women's earnings, 16
    returns for women, 28, 29
Educational attainment, 22–28
    of African American women, 65–70
Elderly women, and poverty, 53–54
Elected officials, women, 39–43
Employment, by sex, 30–31
Entrepreneurship, *see* Business world, women in
Equal Employment Opportunity Commission, 74
Equal Pay Act, 73, 79
Equality of opportunity, 4–5, 79
Equality of outcomes, 4–5, 74, 75
Executive positions, women in, xix, 19–20, 75, 80

Female-headed households, 54, 57–58
Feminization of poverty, 53
Fitzpatrick, Kellyanne, 44
Fortune 1000 and 500 companies, xviii, 18
Fox-Genovese, Elizabeth, xv, 17

Gender gap in voting, 43–44, 45
Glass ceiling, xviii–xix, 11, 18–22, 80
Glass Ceiling Commission, xiv, xv, 18–20, 33, 36
Godbey, Geoffrey, 47n27
Goldin, Claudia, xx, 15, 32
Government intervention, 59–60, 75–76
Gramm, Wendy Lee, 47n37

Henderson, Laura, xxi
Herzberger, Sharon D., 6n2
Hirsch, Barry, 14
Household management, 30

Illegitimacy, 54, 56, 57
Institute for Women's Policy Research, 13
Ireland, Patricia, 7n5

Juhn, Chinhui, 16

Korenman, Sanders, 15
Korn/Ferry, xviii, 19
Kosters, Marvin, 47n26

Labor force, participation in
    by women, 27–32
Lawyers, women, 16–17
Life expectancy, 52–53
Lynch, Michael, 21

Macpherson, David, 14
Male-dominated
    occupations, women in, 34–36
    professions, women in, 19–20
Marital status of women, 56
Marriage, postponed by women, 54, 55
Married women, in labor force, 32
Men, and family responsibilities, 17–18
Mincer, Jacob, 16
Murphy, Kevin, 16

National Association of Women Business Owners, 74
National Foundation of Women Business Owners, 37
National Organization for Women, 11
National Women's Political Caucus, 40
Neumark, David, 15
Newman, Jody, 40
Nossel, Suzanne, 16–17

Occupational choice, women's, 33–36
Occupational segregation, 34–36
O'Melveny, Mary K., 7n5
O'Neill, June, xvii, xx, 14, 36
One-parent households, 56, 58
One-person households, 54
Oster, Sharon, 12

Personal choice, *see* Choices, personal
Pink-collar jobs, 36
Pink ghetto, xviii, xix–xx, 33–36
Pipeline theory, xviii, xix, 19
Political arena, women in, 39–43
Post, Katherine, 21
Poverty
    rates by sex, 52
    and the elderly, 53–54
    and women, 51–58

Powers, Elizabeth, 6n3
Price Waterhouse v. *Hopkins*, 4

Rhode, Deborah, 6n3, 33
Robinson, John, 47n27

Satel, Sally, 60n1
Small Business Administration, xx, 38
Smeal, Eleanor, 34
Smith Barney, 7n5
Sommers, Christina Hoff, 6n3
State officials, women, 39, 41, 43
Statistics, use in charging
        discrimination, 76
Steinem, Gloria, 6n2
Strossen, Nadine, 6n2, 7n5

Temporary Assistance for Needy
        Families, 53, 59–60

Title VII of Civil Rights Act of 1964,
        73–74
Tobias, Sheila, 6n2

Unemployment rates, 21

Voting patterns, of women, 43–45

Wage gap, xvii–xix, 11–17, 80
    for African Americans, 65
Waldfogel, Jane, 14
Wallace, Geoffrey, 59–60
Walsh, Deborah, 39
Welfare reform, and women, 59–60
Westfall, Elizabeth, 16–17
Women
    changing status of, 3–4
    as victims, 5–6, 73, 79, 80
    See also African American women
Women-owned businesses, xxi, 37–38

About the Authors

Diana Furchtgott-Roth is a resident fellow at the American Enterprise Institute and a member of the National Advisory Board of the Independent Women's Forum. She earned an M.Phil. in economics from Oxford University in 1982. Before joining AEI in 1993, Ms. Furchtgott-Roth was the deputy executive secretary of the Domestic Policy Council and later associate director in the Office of Policy Planning at the White House under President Bush. She served on the staff of President Reagan's Council of Economic Advisers from 1986 to 1987.

Christine Stolba is a Ph.D. candidate in history at Emory University, where her research centers on American intellectual history and women's history. An instructor at Emory, she has received a Mellon Research Fellowship for research at the American Philosophical Society and is a member of the American Historical Association and the Historical Society. She has presented her research findings at numerous conferences, including the 1998 meeting of the Organization of American Historians, and has contributed essays to *Women in World History.*